UNDER ORDERS

A SPIRITUAL HANDBOOK
FOR MILITARY PERSONNEL

UNDER ORDERS

A SPIRITUAL HANDBOOK FOR MILITARY PERSONNEL

CHAPLAIN
WILLIAM McCOY

ACW Press
Ozark, AL 36360

UNDER ORDERS: a spiritual Handbook for military personnel
Copyright ©2005 William McCoy
All rights reserved

Cover Design by Alpha Advertising
Interior Design by Pine Hill Graphics

Packaged by ACW Press
1200 HWY 231 South #273
Ozark, AL 36360
www.acwpress.com
The views expressed or implied in this work do not necessarily reflect those of ACW Press. Ultimate design, content, and editorial accuracy of this work is the responsibility of the author(s).

Library of Congress Cataloging-in-Publication Data
(Provided by Cassidy Cataloguing Services, Inc.)

McCoy, William.

    Under orders : a spiritual handbook for military personnel / William
McCoy. -- 1st ed. -- Ozark, AL : ACW Press, 2005.

    p. ; cm.
    ISBN: 1-932124-50-0

    1. Spiritual life. 2. Christian life. 3. Soldiers--Religious life 4.
Soldiers--Conduct of life. I. Title.

BV4501.3 .M33 2005
248.4--dc22   0504

Printed in the United States of America.

*Everyone who achieves great things does so
with the support of hidden other people
who love them and support their vision.
My wife is one of those people.
Everyone should be so fortunate as me.
Winter weekends writing this book,
a year and a half at war as it lay on the shelf,
the loneliness at home and
personal heartache of losses and uncertainty,
all blended together to form a very difficult road
to completion of this project.*

*Through all this she earned the title of a "soldier's wife."
Thanks Carol.*

All photographs used in this book are courtesy of the Defense Visual Information Services (DVIS) and are classified "Released" by that agency. None of the persons pictured in the photos necessarily endorse any of the material written in this book and are pictured solely for the benefit of providing a sense of military life in general. If any individual is identifiable the decision to use the photo is my own and does not suggest that individual's endorsement of this product.

All material in this book is my own opinion and in no way reflects the policy or opinion of the Evangelical Lutheran Church in America, the United States Military or Department of Defense, or the U.S. Army Chaplaincy.

Contents

Know the Terrain, the Seas, the Skies—Understand yourself and everything else will start to make sense.

> Self-awareness and understanding help to make the task of human spirituality less of a mystery and more of a journey. Many times the spiritual problems we have are the result of our own difficulty with perfection rather than our unwillingness to believe. Accepting who we are and how we're made is a first step toward living true spirituality. It's not perfection but intent that is so important.

Be Confident. You are made out of the right stuff despite what your boss says and what you feel.

> Rather than debunking a generation of youthful minds and hearts, this chapter seeks to validate the notoriously ribald and unashamedly direct postmoderns and integrate their viewpoints into the dialogue about God. This is done through illustrating their contributions and intelligence. This brings them into the dialogue rather than requiring them to become something they are not—a stand-alone rule that postmoderns are right to hold.

Believe in God. God has one face and many followers so why is there confusion?

> It is hard for many people to accept that there can be many ways for people to believe in God. But having faith in God is something that cannot be just for one religious group. Albeit Christian faith heralds Jesus Christ as the Savior of the world, there are many good people in the world seeking after God. This validates religious experience as a good step toward being human. It encourages thought and speculation.

This is all about the presuppositions of faith and where belief begins. Questions are where faith begins, not where it ends. Tough questions require us to smash through the assumptions we live under, and enable us to rise up and make the best decisions about a personal faith.

It is often true that the closest thing to God we will ever know is some human being. This is all about the great people who do pass through our lives and help us to picture God. I encourage the reader to let go of the negative people and embrace the good people, the people who do seem to bring God into their lives. We should never allow bad people to get in our way of knowing God.

Probably one of the three most important issues for 18 to 25-year-old thinkers today is what happens to me at death and what is my significance in the world as a result. Using one of the great novels of Simone de Beauvoir, I illustrate the necessity of being a human being with a limited existence and how this is really merciful of God to us. We are designed to be limited and this shouldn't be the end for us. Life comes in phases, and we should manage each phase carefully. It is all eventually about hope for the future that brings life to us.

The age-old problem of sin is undertaken in a way to enable the reader to understand it without defining sin for each person. Ultimately, there is no list of sins any greater than another list. We all have specific issues with regard to our sin both personally and judicially before God. We should realize that sin is normal and is the reason we are entitled to God's grace so freely. Without sin, we'd be perfect. It is part of our makeup and we must understand it to live better.

INTRODUCTION
to the Idea of Under Orders

He could have been any one of us. A Roman soldier was troubled about the condition of his servant. The servant was dying and the soldier had exhausted all possible cures for him. Perhaps he had heard there was a prophet in town and thought maybe he'd try asking that prophet for help. He didn't have to be religious, and probably wasn't. He was military.

His life consisted of obeying orders. He probably didn't have a lot of extra income to help his servant. His last attempt was to see the prophet Jesus. When he found Jesus, Jesus told him that his servant was already healed. He believed the prophet and explained that he didn't need to go home to verify this miracle, all he had to do was to follow the order for he was a soldier "under orders" and understood how the military command structure functioned. Jesus' command that day probably changed the soldier's life. Perhaps in no other profession is it easier to understand this story than the military profession.

Military personnel number nearly two million today. For most of them, religion and faith were things they shoved to the back of their minds when they entered the military. Yet despite that, religion remains one of their chief concerns. And in battle, no one laughs at a soldier receiving a blessing when the chaplain wades through the casualties. Service men and women share this unusual relationship with this Roman soldier that they can understand spiritual things clearer than other people. Perhaps that is due to the inherent danger of their job, or due to the understanding of authority, or perhaps because they find themselves often with time on their hands to think about it so often. Night watches aboard, check-post duties, patrols, first up hooches for medevac and emergency response teams, and so many similar obscure yet essential jobs put our service men and women in a lonely category far away from their homes, culture and churches that might have sent them off to that world. These people are the forgotten of the church while at the same time the parish for chaplains of all services.

This is a book about all the service men and women of the armed forces who even now provide security, pull watches and go where ordered to go despite the dangers, regardless of the pay, holding back their fears to forge a new world free of terror. These are the forgotten heroes on the cutting edge of an uncertain future. They are changing our world right now in the war against terrorism. Now more than ever the military is becoming one of the most challenging and demanding jobs our nation offers young men and women right out of high school. Operation Iraqi Freedom alone has nearly 150,000 soldiers deployed to stabilize a country which is still in the throes of anarchy after the deposition of Saddam Hussein. Reservists and Guardsmen are facing back-to-back deployments and durations of up to eighteen months away from home. How can these individuals hold on to faith or discover faith in such turbulence? Who is speaking to this heroic post 9-11 generation who are prosecuting the war against terror? They are a generation of young people in the prime of their lives, deployed far away from home at airbases and aboard ships in surging seas where normal is some strange daily existence to which they have to conform. In spite of the hardships, there is a need for a handbook on spirituality and spiritual things to help this generation understand both themselves and the larger reality of God around them. I hope this book finds its way into the cargo pockets, C-bags, pea coats and flight jackets all across this nation and our world as they struggle to understand how their faith and life works in this ominously turbulent time.

This is also a book about an entire generation of young people who have been assessed, labeled and shoved into sociological categories so that *whatever* they might try to say or do, they are never quite right. At the same time, they are the brave prosecutors of the current war on terrorism, the techno smart kids of MTV and the "alternative" and misunderstood kids of a generation now mysteriously and arrogantly labeled "postmodern." This is about all those bright people who now serve in our armed forces who are anywhere from 17 to 25 years old. It is a handbook to think through one's faith about, to reflect about one's choices with, and to guide those people as they create the new world ahead. It will be sometimes tough and difficult to work through to that world. It will be a bit intellectual at times and then it will be real personal at other times. The bottom line is that this work is both general in how it speaks to a generation and intensely personal when it speaks to individuals.

I too am part of a generation shaped by an emerging modern world after World War Two.[1] I guess even my kids would

---

[1] At the end of World War II existentialism was the philosophy of the day. Now at the beginning of the twenty-first century, postmodernism is giving birth to new shapes and thinking about the world, and about God. American young people in the service returned from the war in Europe to build homes and start families on the verge of an incredible economic boom. The boom continues world-wide and even the strike on the World Trade Center and the estimated eight billion dollar slowdown it caused only slowed the trading day of the US economy. Yet in spite of our robust economic outlook, our centers of spiritual gravity are being replaced by mutual fund security, jobs, travel and the remoteness of combat. All the while, the same generational age of people who left Europe in 1945 are today deployed in over sixty countries of the world in an effort to sustain our way of life.

say I'm pretty predictable, not many surprises to my life. Anyway, I went through the crazy sixties, the Vietnam years and into college. I knew pretty much the career path I would take, I took it, and I'm still in it. I hope I will retire in so many years and have made my world a little better place than it was when it was handed to me by my parents, the "Greatest Generation." Although that title is well-deserved and honorific, it irritates me that it is used only in reference to my folks. In turn, I think the generation about which this book is written is truly the "next greatest generation," as bright, as courageous and filled with insights as my folks, my generation and everyone who reads this.

If it weren't for the labels we put on each generation, we might enjoy being ourselves a bit more and have more confidence in our contributions to our world and society. I hope those people who are serving our country will take note that they are the subject of this work. And I think they are an articulate and astute group. Yet they also hunger for things that all of us should want. They want reality, truth, honesty, sincerity and purpose just like I did in the 1960s and like my parents were raised to uphold in the 1920s. But for whatever reason, their voices are rarely heard over the hubbub of my generation, whose concern is more often a reaction rather than a reception of ideas.

And that is a concern for me. As a chaplain in the U.S. Army and as a former kid myself, I think this entire generation is about to shape a new world. I also think it is time to stop and listen to their language and thoughts and attempt to work with them to understand the God about which they are trying to formulate words and ideas.

In a sense, our images and understanding of God are generational. Every generation owes it to themselves to translate what they know about God into their own language. This book is that attempt. And en route to that description, I hope to provide to each individual who reads it the "starting point" for their intellectual and spiritual quest. I do not think the religious or philosophic labels of the past are sufficient to explain the future. But I think the issues, the questions and the concerns are mostly identical.

I do think my generation needs to realize the emerging new world and attempt to provide this generation the best tools possible in discovering it. In a very literal sense, my generation is passing away and the modern world which went with the cold war period is now gone. I am now a product of the "postmodern" world and thinking myself. But I too am a bridge from one generation to another. If I don't somehow "break down" the images I under-stand of God or the language used about God for this generation, they will turn against me and ask me why I was so generic and didn't want to be specific. So I will be specific and sometimes direct. And ultimately, I will seek here to connect timeless ideas and truths with a generation labeled "extreme" junkies.

The book follows the simple format of ten easy-to-understand "orders." Within these ten orders I take the reader to the key issues that soldiers tell me are hot topics for them. Read in any order you find works for you. Lots of times the military life has these "waiting periods" that find us with lots of time on our hands and little to do. I wanted to make sure that not only would the service men and women find the orders interesting, but that there is additional material in footnotes and in the "Considerations" at the end of each chapter which will provide them lots of thinking time.

Too, this book can be used as a group effort for discussion making it a reference and a program for leaders. I envision airmen and sailors huddling in small groups now and then to discuss and spar about the topics my considerations promote. Again let me state, there are a million answers in the world but it is perhaps the greatest strength to be able to ask the right questions in dialogue. Questions have a way of purifying our logic and bringing us into confrontation with our false assumptions about God, our lives and the people with whom we interact. But more about that in the chapter on "Questions."

Most of all, I hope the servicemen and servicewomen who read this book will pick up on my Christian hope. In the midst of this world I find the Gospel reassures me that despite whose religious position may win persuasion on news programs or whose politics gains a groundswell of opinion in the world, the Gospel, not religion, holds a key for everyone in its basic law of love. And that is the secret of this book. If you don't read any of it, read the last chapter and find out who "wins." It's not the most powerful, or the most successful, or the most good-looking. The one who wins is the one who loses everything for the sake of others—noble sacrifice.

This ultimate law is based in the Judaeo-Christian concept of sacrifice. Despite the cries for economic parity by current religious extremists, what is more important is that each individual know the importance of his or her life in the perspective of his or her neighbor. Ultimately, we will be judged by our fellowman and by God by the way we treat our neighbors and our enemies. An old Jewish concept of reciprocity requires that we cannot be right with God and wrong with each other. The ultimate law of love brings us all to the same table of justice with the same requirements for each other.

This book may disturb the close-minded thinker and it might challenge conventional ideas about your beliefs. It may not appeal to the self-absorbed and then it may—that depends on their openness. It might be snatched up by the curious and the troubled. Great. But that we subject ourselves to reading something that is a little out of our league, out of our comfort zone, is my objective. And once we interact with the ideas here, if we go out and attempt to put them into practice we may in fact change ourselves and renew our world.

Ultimately, I hope we will bring the good news to our world, not my good news, but the good news of the Gospel!

ORDER ONE

**Know the Terrain, the Seas, the Skies—
Understand yourself and everything else
will start to make sense.**

"You can do anything you put your mind to..."

Eminem, from "8 Mile"

THE MOST COMMON PROBLEM FOR EVERYONE

Who are you? Socrates told his students they should first of all "know themselves." You are probably the toughest puzzle you'll ever encounter in life. And yet the more you piece yourself together the clearer the world will get. Many of the service men and women I counsel are totally confused about religion, faith, their purpose in the world, their broken relationships, because they have no clue as to who they are. The first questions they should ask are about themselves.

Probably one of the biggest problems with spirituality and religion is that people tend to search for themselves by shopping religions. When that happens they define themselves from some point beyond themselves. It would be really helpful if we started by understanding why it is we want certain things for our spirituality. Then search or "shop" for our spiritual "comfort zone" in religion. Find out who I am and why I want certain things out of my searching. That search is often religious, but takes on emotional searches, sexual quests, job advancement (usually in older adults who like to destroy others and win the best job positions for themselves).

I will bounce from speaking to you as a person, to speaking about this "next generation" terminology. I do that because I think everyone is unique yet I admit that we tend to belong to groups of thinkers called "generations" for lack of a better word. It is characteristic of this generation that it doesn't want to be labeled and so I will bounce.

Every person with whom I come into contact in the Army has some sort of identity. All of those identities are not necessarily final. Many people seem to "try on" various styles of identity before settling on a preferred one.

Jenny (fictitious name) is typical of that identity crisis. Raised in a haphazard home environment, a father who would come and go, and a mother addicted to crack, Jenny and her sister lived in an old car from day to day. Her mother had numerous sexual relationships and from time to time would pawn off either her or her sister to a suitor. Jenny's father also sexually abused her and her sister. Jenny *seemed* to survive the ordeal, finally being shuffled into foster homes. After repeated beatings and sexual abuse in foster homes she arrived in a stable home to complete her high school years. When she showed up in the Navy she was determined to do better than her mother and make something of herself. She soon realized that many of the same people she had left behind were now standing beside her in basic training.

When she showed up in the chapel office she detailed a horrific story of survival from sexual abuse at the hands of her father, imprisonment of her mother, institutionalization of her sister. She was still attractive and wore her uniform sharply but her life was a mess. She couldn't tell the truth and would cry in order to shape her request for help. She announced plans for marriage and was soon off to get married. I cautioned her a bit about marriage, knowing myself that she didn't have much of a chance to succeed, but encouraged her as much as I could and we parted.

Some time later, Jenny reappeared, tearful and determined to beat the system. She was leaving her young soldier husband for another man or two, she was being judicially punished by the Uniform Code of Military Justice for being AWOL and she had no intention of surviving to be better than her mother. In fact, she was repeating all the mistakes she had learned in that car. She eventually left the military with no resolution except that in her own mind she thought things would be better somewhere else outside the military. She is probably still searching as you read this.

Jenny is repeated a hundred times over in our military service branches. She couldn't break free of her habits because she had no idea who she was. She was committing the same mistakes as her mother because she had never slowed down long enough to get help with her situation, her view of herself, and the way she would fit into the military and the world. Wearing a uniform is one thing. Changing the inner soul is another.

Jenny typifies the identity crisis that seems rampant in this generation. Right now, more than ever before, young men and women are having to carve out their identities in the midst of a turbulent world. Add to that the disrupted home lives out of which they come from and you have a uniform wrapped around a body and mind that seems sometimes far from rationality. What makes an identity and how can we find our place in this world, so to speak?

Things are made even more difficult by the fact that the world in which this generation lives isn't like the one in which I grew up in. Add to that the fact that what seemed reasonable to me thirty years ago has no semblance of relevance to people like Jenny today. But how are people like Jenny or the next sailor to be expected to understand themselves in this world? All the expectations are gone. Today we don't expect that every kid graduating from high school comes from a Beaver Cleaver family. In reality, most families are broken or breaking. Marriage is not reliable. Divorce is common. How could Jenny be expected to do anything less than leave her husband when times were confusing?

PERSONAL INVENTORY AND MAKEUP

Seems to me that all service members would do well to perform an initial inventory on their personal lives. That inventory ought to be somewhat formalized. In other words, rather than just graduating from high school and entering the service wide-eyed, every young man and woman ought to go through a checklist for personal awareness. Just like we would perform a battle drill or pre-battle checklist, perform a personal awareness checklist for my own self.

It is alarming how few people really take the time to do this sort of thing. Yet, when someone in the unit purchases a new vehicle, there is no end to reading of the manual, cleaning and polishing and tinkering with the thing. But time after time in my office it is the same look, that blank stare, that often surprises someone when I ask about their background, their family, their choices. It's like they haven't a clue that all of this plays into the current dilemma they face. And yet it does. Most problems I encounter are the result of things that happened years ago. Few soldiers realize this.

Despite the current postmodern generational label, all generations are the same at this point—they are products of their environment, the people and ideas they've encountered, and the choices they make. Most of them focus on their developmental environment while most of my work lies in getting them to make another choice. Yet in the midst of it the most glaring item missing is the person's failure to properly identify themselves. And that may not be such an easy process. Let's begin.

Fundamentally, every person is put together in terms of those elements I just mentioned but those feed into what I call a three-dimensional humanness: the body, the soul and the spirit. This is not new. It actually comes out of Classicism as the Greeks and then later the enlightenment thinkers tried to assimilate how a human being was defined. First, we have to understand this three-dimensional aspect. The physical body is a given. Everyone is born, lives and dies. The soul is often a synonym for spirit, but I prefer to think of the soul in that sense in which it embodies the thinking aspect of a person. Also I like to think that the place from which our choices come, our volition, lies within that soul. It is the part I most identify with when I say "me." The spirit is my eternal aspect. The spirit is that essential part of me which defines me as being spiritual rather than just dust and dirt. We often suggest that animals have bodies and perhaps some sense of souls but no spirit. That's why there is a doggie heaven right?

Rather than haggle about two or three parts of a human being, I will settle with this three-part idea. It really doesn't matter too much whether we mix soul and spirit together in the long run but for clarity, it might help you to look at yourself as a three-part being.

YOUR PHYSICAL MAKEUP

The body is a fascinating aspect of being a human because it is the thing in which we perform all the things we do. If you have done anything in your life, you did it with that body. We "do" things with our bodies. We take the body along for the ride. It is critical that you understand that your physical body can interact with your soul at points too. Like when you go to the medic and they inform you that you have an STD, you realize that the choices you made impacted your physical body with a second or third effect despite your wishes. That can be a wake-up call for some people that stirs them to change their habits and in so doing, affects their souls and their bodies from that time forward.

Bodies in today's generation are the subject of much awareness in videos and film. There is a preoccupation with the sensing of pain and the essential need for individuals to feel things in their bodies in order for them to really know something. The body is not just a vehicle but is a message board. Tattoos are the rage today and provide the person an artistic tableau on which to surface issues, signal allegiances, and make promises evident on their surface rather than just on the inside. Tattoos were a big subject around my house for some time as all three of my teenagers surged through the process.

I wanted for some time to view tattoos as a stage they were going through but kept out of it and watched what happened instead. I reminded them all that once they graduated from high school they could tattoo right up to their eyelids, that it was their body and their choice. Today, all three of my children have expressive tattoos. I don't have any. It's just that my generation didn't express in the way this one expresses. I don't think there is anything particularly "wrong" with tattoos but think they really tell us where a person is coming from. If they need to tattoo, that is their option. But the body they are tattooing is part of who they are. And so, the tattoos seem to be reflective of some very earnest feelings.

One of my sons, who is now an Air Force Pararescueman, had always loved flames. He loved flames so much that he asked if he could "flame-out" the Malibu "beater" car he drove to high school. I said sure, and he implemented a flame design on the hood. We all were quite humored with the flames on the beater. Some years later he had those same flames tattooed on his shoulders along with many other images signifying his orientation to God, his cultural roots and his expectations in life. We still chuckle about the Malibu.

The body is a vehicle for self-awareness. The body is the way I get myself into situations that help and hurt me. I experience the world through my body. Yet for all its capabilities I still find young people only scratching the surface as to its capabilities. There are a lot of piercings (pain orientation and a uniqueness sign) yet not so many of this generation are working to make the body a better transport device. That's where substance abuse enters and creates havoc.

Not only could the body be an enhanced vehicle of awareness but it could be honed to perfection with fitness and training. Not that we ought to return to a classical Grecian form here, but soldiers and sailors would do themselves well to ask whether or not they are missing out on the benefits of a healthy vehicle by ingesting the ingredients in drugs like ecstasy. Bodily fitness can enhance our situational awareness and provide us the capacity to sustain ourselves in combat, to build our long-term immune capability, and keep us from degrading into over-weight complications. It also functions hand in glove with the functions of our souls.

YOUR SOUL MAKEUP

The souls work with the body. The soul, being the mind, the volition, the thinking and rationale that make us human, is tied to the body like an egg and shell. Yet in the soul are all the elements for true power often left untapped by most of the people I talk to. My father, a veteran of thirty years in the Army, and still a sharp mind at 83, recently fell ill. After only several hours of fever his mind lapsed into dullness. We nursed him through a week of delirium before seeing his soul reappear. The way we interact with voice and eyes all comes from the soul and is carried by the body. Hurt the body and the soul has a difficult time of rising to any occasion.

Our souls are quite capable faculties for self-awareness and are often accused of doing things all on their own. Many times, our human awareness is handicapped by our one-dimensional view of ourselves. I have often heard service members tell me about things they were doing and choices they were making and yet when I tried to connect the body and soul together I just got a funny look back. Think about it, if you take your new car and drive it through the doors into the base exchange you will probably hurt it, right? Then ask yourself how stupid you'll look when the military police come up to your window and peer in and ask you what you are doing. You can't separate what you do with your body, your vehicle for human expression, and your soul, your thinking. They go hand in hand.

And there is more. The functions of the soul that define us are things like self-esteem, self-assurance, self-awareness, self-respect and so forth. Our reasoning comes from the soul as does our ability to analyze decisions of the past and learn from them. The soul is powerful yet we often disregard its voice like it is junk mail or something.

The soul is an inner world of thoughts and discussion that becomes our "review board" for decision making and for our personal assessment of our life. Some inner worlds are better than others, we find out.

A personal checklist for yourself might include the following questions:

Am I the last person on earth? Realize that you aren't the first person to think the way you do. This will encourage you when things are tough. And this will help you understand that life is much bigger than you. Knowing others have faced stuff helps you to bear up under the load and make it.

Am I on trial here? Remember that your conscience functions like a kangaroo court sometimes and you may need to correct its ways before thinking you did the right thing. Lots of people today don't have reliable consciences because theirs were never developed adequately to function as a good arbiter between right and wrong. Watch out for giving yourself bad advice. Check your conscience with people smarter than you or people that appear to you to be "on the ball."

Do I have all the answers yet? Read, Read, Read. And don't just read the Internet. Read the stuff people talk about in life. If you missed this in school then start reading now. Books like *The Grapes of Wrath*, *The Pickwick Papers*, *Moby Dick*, the Bible, and others, are part of a huge reading list, which if you fail to read you will miss directions for the rest of your life. Books hold lessons wrapped in stories that tell you where the potholes in life are, so to speak. All the answers are in the books.

Am I a religious or spiritual person? Pray. You don't have to be a chaplain or a minister to make a prayer. Praying is a function of human beings. All cultures, tribes, and nations pray. Most Americans (80 percent) believe in a god of some kind. Then start praying. Prayer has been known to assist in the recovery of patients in hospitals and is a way of self-healing as well. When you talk to God something happens in your body and in your soul. Healing begins.

Who am I? Identify your family or what parts of a family you find you belong to the most. Embrace who you are fearlessly. Be proud of where you came from to get where you are today. Work to identify the best things about your family and your "people." Black military service members can often be heard talking about their "people" and sometimes other races become indignant about this exclusivism. But the fact is, each of us has his or her "people" yet we haven't learned to embrace and identify with our "people." Start simple but find your place in this long history of human beings. Be that and be it well for all to see.

Where am I going in life? Vast numbers of people have no idea where they are going with their life decisions. Life is a game of good or bad plays in a video game and some win and others don't. And yet it isn't just the plays, but where to go with your plays. Life has moral consequences that grow out of your choices so that where you are going is often determined by the decisions you make. You often define yourself by those decisions. If you are being driven by an agenda you are not aware of, you may be shaking your head wondering how you got there when you arrive at your destination!

YOUR SPIRITUAL MAKEUP

Back to Jenny. If for one moment Jenny had attempted to break free of the bonds of the expectations she lived under to do some personal inventory she might have had a chance to break her addiction to pathological lying and misbehavior. What the military could never help Jenny with was herself. Only Jenny could do that. Given the chance to reorganize her thinking, she squandered that opportunity. The military only gives us one or maybe two chances at the very best to recover from our mistakes in life. After making repeated mistakes, the military finally adjudicated Jenny's behavior in the unwavering terms of the military code of justice. She was busted to a Seaman from a Seaman 3rd class, had to pay two months salary back to the military, was put on extra duty for forty-five days buffing floors, weeding and picking up trash, and was "chaptered" out of the military with a less than honorable discharge (that follows her the rest of her working life and biases employers against her).

Had Jenny taken only a moment to sit down and reassess her life patterns and ask herself why she believed what she did about herself, and then looked for professional help with those questions, she might have changed the course of her life. As it turned out, Jenny took the road that most "uniformed" young people take. She failed to know herself and became fodder for the cannons of military justice. There is very little anyone can do for a person who doesn't want to help themselves. And there is less help if that person doesn't know who they are.

Fundamentally, everyone is spiritual, yet that aspect of their humanness rarely comes to mind. People don't sit around and think about their spirituality. Yet our spirituality is always with us, part of our inner beings, and something which is carried from one place to another, either wittingly or unwittingly. Your spirituality is part of the way I believe God makes you as you enter the world. Because it is part of your nature, it will never demand anything,  it will always lie within you as a possibility—like options on a new car you never know about because you've never read the new car manual. Quite a thought isn't it? There's something more to you than you realized.

considerations

Consideration 1: What is the "thing" that makes us incapable of being honest with ourselves when the only person we cannot lie to is ourselves? Seems like fear of facing ourselves is the most scary thing in life . Most of us state that we will never be like our parents. Jenny was terrified of becoming like her mother and yet she was identical. She couldn't face up to what her mother was in her own actions. Fear of what we will find within ourselves keeps us often from doing anything about our lives. Fear paralyzes. Can you identify the control agent in your life?

Consideration 2: Is the body meaningful for my life? Well, you can't live without it! But seriously, the physical body has always had a lot of discussion in the history of philosophy. It is more than just a vehicle. One Marine had come into the maxillofacial surgical unit at Tripler Hospital in Hawaii and told the oral surgeons that he had joined the Marines because of the way he looked. After a year of jaw realignment and teeth straightening he was a male model and remarked to the staff that he was getting out of the service and wanted to go to the university and make something more of his life. He thought that his body was restricting his choices in life. In reality, they were! He had decided that his looks defined himself. This is probably more true of us than anything else I know. But our bodies shouldn't hold that kind of sway over us. How has your body determined your habits or your choices in life?

Consideration 3: Can you feed a soul? We feed everything else, I guess so! Sure the soul can be nourished. I estimate that it is malnourished in most people though. I often wonder about the steady diet of material we feed to the soul in terms of the things we take in to our life. Going back to the Gospels, Jesus said that it wasn't what went into a person that defiled him but what came out that did so. However, most of the material which goes in produces very little in quality output when it comes out of our life. Military people are probably the most in touch with this characteristic though as they are very acquainted with the process of getting information, rules, orders and battle drills into their minds. Upon order they can spit out anything the chief or sergeant wants from them. Take this a step further and ask yourself what sort of material are you putting into your emotional, spiritual and intellectual life?

ORDER TWO

Be Confident—You are made out of the right stuff despite what your boss says and what you feel.

"Run Forrest, Run!"
the endlessly quoted phrase from the movie *"Forrest Gump"*

A FIREFIGHT IN AFGHANISTAN TELLS THE STORY BEST:

During the battle of Sha-i-khot in Afghanistan, I kept a close eye on the daily news reports from the Army units engaged in the battle. It gave me a great sense of pride to follow the efforts of the young men and women deployed to Operation Enduring Freedom (OEF) to fight the Taliban in that remote region. My heart was often in my throat as I read the journalist's reports that flowed daily into the Pentagon's "Early Bird," a compilation of newspaper articles.

For the first time since Desert Storm a new generation of soldiers was going off to war. I watched with anticipation to see how they would fare. I was impressed as were many of my colleagues.

What had previously been a generation maligned as Nintendo, MTV couch potatoes, sagging grunge and gothic lost children, had turned into combat soldiers in desert BDUs taking on a fierce and brutal army of wicked religious extremists. And they shredded their enemy.

I was particularly struck by the efforts of one young Army infantry company commander and his men who had become targets of the enemy after landing in a shallow ridgeline in direct-fire sight of the Taliban. As he and his young soldiers were held down by mortar fire from a higher enemy position, the commander kept his cool despite the crack of bullets whizzing past. Because the Taliban held up in a cave when the Air Force fighter jets assaulted their position, they were able to survive each air strike by running into their cave. Periodically they would taunt the soldiers by running out of their cave laughing and jumping up and down. Then they would reset their mortars and lay their fires on the young soldiers. The air strikes did little to impair their firepower.

The shrapnel and enemy fire were often so intense that the company of soldiers could only bury their faces in the gravel hoping to obscure their silhouettes from the enemy's fire. It was reminiscent of the assault of the Allies at Anzio in Italy when the soldiers used their steel pot helmets to etch out an inch or two of the limestone beach to escape the German machine guns. Withering fire, it is called, because it is so endless and deadly.

The captain realized the situation needed a precise plan and figured in order to strike them he would have to time his mortar fires just at the moment the Air Force jets struck the enemy positions (in order to mask the firing of his mortar section). He calculated the seconds needed for a coordinated air strike with mortars firing high into the mountain crag positions of the enemy. When the Taliban ran out of their cave to celebrate this time, they were met with the arrival of the U.S. mortar rounds that had been fired only thirty seconds before, masked by the Air Force jets' pounding. Unaware of any mortar firing from the ground, the Taliban met their creator rather jubilantly yet unexpectedly.

As the Taliban had taken its toll on this small unit, these brave teenage soldiers wrapped wounds to arms, legs and faces and fought on. Their courage was undaunting. I was impressed by the accounts of their bravery and grateful for their sacrifice. I wondered whether I would have been as brave. Their young commander enabled them to find that magic moment, assault and subdue the enemy. The entire company survived the ordeal. A moment as fine as any scene from *Saving Private Ryan* played out by a generation most consider totally self-absorbed and disinterested in important things—a postmodern generation of soldiers!

Yet these soldiers are only one of a thousand stories of courage from a generation of youth no one of my generation expected to rise to the occasion of military service. A generation raised on *Star Wars*, Austin Powers and MTV has risen to the ranks of military service and are doing well at it. When asked if the soldiers wanted to return to another fight after being shot up on the ridgeline—to a man, they grabbed their gear and energetically loaded the helicopter for another trip into the deadly snow-covered mountain peaks.

THE "NEXT GENERATION"

I am especially impressed with this "next generation" of service men and women. The events of September 11 have given this generation a reason to belong and an opportunity to make their mark for generations to come. Along with that mark I often have wondered whether we've done all for them we should. In the time my generation has grown up as beneficiaries of the Second World War, the world has changed. Perspectives are not the same. The service members of today with their tattoos, piercings and alternative views is not just another generation and can hardly be labeled correctly by any sociological study. What we do know is they are as remarkable a generation as they are bold, brave and courageous. They are every bit as impressive as their grandparents of Tom Brokaw's "Greatest Generation" were in World War II. Yet they rarely have received credit for what they're made of.

Today, unlike the days of Vietnam, a new generation is heading off to war in support of Operation Enduring Freedom and Operation Iraqi Freedom. In my own family, every grandchild of my veteran father is in the military. They represent each branch of the service—Army, Navy, Marines, Air Force and Coast Guard. I have often asked whether I've done all I could to prepare these young brave family members for the eventuality of combat operations. Yet even more I wonder how this brave generation will shape the world to come, what kind of interpretation will they bring to their war when it is over, and what kind of spirituality will sustain them until that time?

This is a heroic generation. At no other time has a generation been so labeled and scrutinized, and often maligned though. Being a Baby Boomer was a fun sort of sociological label for my generation. Sure we had our 1960s revolution, anti-war movement, Jesus movement, drugs, alcohol and sexual experimentation. But after shaking up our world, we quickly returned to its norms, expectations and found ourselves returning to the foundations of our culture, our spiritual traditions. With some modifications, we figured that involvement in the "system" was by far a more effective means of shaping the world and ourselves than revolution. The Boomers have been the focus of a plethora of studies but are now the sort of start-point for an endless succession of new assessment criteria about Xers, Yers and a host of alternative qualifiers. I'm not so sure anyone in this next generation cares too much about the assessments being made upon them.

Perhaps it is an American sociological trait to want to label in order to understand a generation. And maybe too it is a hope our society has to somehow control a generation who seem to be breaking the expectations of my generation and that of my parents, the World War Two cohort. Whatever it is, I find a great resistance amongst my generation to accept this next generation and its perspectives. And when it comes to spirituality, it appears that my generation does not understand the language of today. It also seems as though this current generation has been disenfranchised of faith because they cannot connect with the structures or concepts of faith that have been passed on to them. This wouldn't be the first time in history that faith lost its relevance for a generation though. But it seems that today's generation rages differently about life and when it does, it gets a disappointing look from the established clergy.

As an Army chaplain and Lutheran minister, I see things otherwise. I think we owe it to ourselves to listen to this generations' comments about our culture and spirituality and seek to understand their voice. If the current war on terrorism has taught us anything it is that the world has completely changed and we have not turned over to this next generation a world that can be considered normal. Unlike my generation who inherited a booming culture of growth and personal gratification in the West, this generation has inherited a terrifying and bizarre future, a pallid tapestry of questionable values, irrational choices and cultural estrangement. They cannot sleep so peacefully at night as I did in the happy 1950s. They are saddled with the redemption of civilized order and the shaking of paradigms. Their world has been rocked. Their options are minimal. They may not have a future. Nor may we.

In this world of questionable options they enter as the heroes on a ridgeline under fire. Yet for what? What can inspire them to hope in the future? Is it possible to give them an answer to their ubiquitous "whatever" expression? Do the norms and baselines of the past give them any hope for the future? In this time the paradigms are not shifting, they are breaking. Old paradigms are not being replaced with traditional new configurations. This isn't Mozart being replaced by Eminem. This is

Mozart breaking apart. This is straight-up a ripping apart of the foundations of thought. And in the midst of the war on terrorism, this generation is taking their evolving paradigm with them.

THIS WORLD IS REALLY A STRANGE PLACE

In metaphoric terms, the difference between what is evolving and what has been is the difference between an old-fashioned kaleidoscope and computerized fractals. Years ago I attended an Episcopal Church conference in New York City whose topic dealt with the curious oddity of computerized fractalization. Though at the time I thought it rather esoteric, I also found that the possibility of emerging random computerized patterns based upon mathematical assumptions and calculations fascinating though irrelevant.

When I was a kid, everyone liked looking through a kaleidoscope. It was nearly the same concept as the computerized fractals except not nearly so sophisticated. Turn the tube and see the pretty patterns evolve. The difference between fractals and the kaleidoscope is that just by shaking of the tube we could produce new images. There is not a clean understandable mathematical or calculable rationality for the changes we are now seeing. Our world is being shaken. We're looking through a wild kaleidoscope today.

What we are seeing today sociologically and spiritually is the rapidly emerging new patterns of alternative ways of seeing the world and our place in it produced by a violent shaking and a rejection of commonly held assumptions. Imagine a Baby Boomer taking the kaleidoscope and shaking up the world and then handing it to the next child who only discovers none of the patterns make any sense. The fractals at least make sense because they are based on assumptions. The assumptions of this culture are gone. This world is shaking and evolving quicker than we can answer for it. That makes it very hard for anyone to look and see any goodness in it, much less God in it.

It is no longer a world of Protestants and Catholics for instance. It is a world of Muslims and Christians, of Jews and Arabs, or Hindus and Sikhs, of commercialists and tribalists, of westerners and western easterners, of uprisings and conflicts. Religion is at conflict in the world, but not just religion alone. Behind the religious uproar is a world of free economies, new merger economies and old communist regimes. It is a world of varying economies—the haves and the have-nots. The European Community is beginning to emerge into a world power of some twenty nations. No longer is the American economy unthreatened. The euro is gaining strength against the dollar and as it does, power seems to be shifting to other centers of influence other than a dollar-based orientation.

The old paradigm of a world locked in cold conflict between two superpowers is out. A world of U.S. military supremacy is being rocked and challenged by nomadic warriors throughout the world hiding behind religious extremism. What is happening is a deliberate breaking of paradigms without a reassembling of them into a conventional redesign. It is an anarchy. Spiritually, the paradigms have been ripped apart and are not being reshaped into some particular Protestant or Catholic option. The young people of this generation are not speaking the language of conventional spirituality and yet in their own way, they are. There is also a religious anarchy in the minds and souls of this next generation.

POSTMODERN AND MILLENNIAL PHILOSOPHY

The emerging world with its new paradigms and its new agendas influences our ways of thinking and communicating. There is a new language and way of understanding the world. And it works for this new world.

Much of this new understanding is based in the postmodern assumptions of this generation. Postmodernism is this generation's philosophic orientation though they don't really care about that label and so I don't choose to use it either.[2] I think it is counterproductive to label without seeking to understand the label. In so many ways this is typical of the modern generation that we must identify, typify and allocate, in order to make "sense" of the present or future. This is like the fractals again. This generation really doesn't want to be called postmodern nor do they care about that generalization. After all, they don't want to be characterized. And that in itself is part of what makes them postmodern. But for the sake of understanding ourselves we need to discover the things which indicate we are postmodern. Because it is my opinion that not only is an emerging generation of service members in this entourage, but we are all caught up in this new thought.

I find that my work with them shows me that the issue at hand is not one of characterization. It really doesn't help a soldier when she comes into my office and I tell her, "Hey, you are a postmodern soldier and your difficulty with the system is due to the fact that you must come to understand the chain of command—they can alter your life, put you on extra duty, and take money out of your monthly pay if you don't straighten out and do what you're supposed to do!" The typical answer to that sort of approach is, "I don't really care about that." It's not because the service member doesn't understand. It is because they speak

---

[2] Postmodernism belongs to the philosophic discussion about the current thought trends of this world. Like existentialism was born out of World War II, postmodernism was born out of the free spirited 60s as successive generations realized that true meaning cannot come from economics nor oblique structures and institutions. Meaning grows out of me, my relationships, my world whether it is orderly or chaotic. Postmoderns reject established patterns and replace them with their random thoughts and ideas. No boundaries exist. "Whatever" is just as authentic as Law. Professor Mary Klages, Assoc. Prof of English at Univ of Colorado at Boulder, states it well, "Postmodernism, in contrast, doesn't lament the idea of fragmentation, provisionality, or incoherence, but rather celebrates that. The world is meaningless? Let's not pretend that art can make meaning then, let's just play with nonsense."

a different language in their concept of the emerging world. And they honestly believe that their viewpoint is critically important in the mix. And it is.

Yet it isn't complete without identifying the fact that this postmodern way of talking and making choices in life comes from a philosophic trend that began in the modern post-existentialist world.[3] The names associated with this in the university are writers and thinkers from Europe like, Hans Georg Gadamer, Jacques Derrida, Edmond Husserl, Jean Merleau-Ponty, to name a few. Postmodern thinkers aren't godless, they are trying to formulate new ways of understanding! What filters down from the halls of the university to high school, into television and magazine cultural outlets, is the "street version" postmodernism. Elements of deconstructionism (a very philosophic way of saying "break it down") are pervasive in our world culture. It is even telling that the Taliban extremists are essentially postmodern Muslims, creating international havoc. There is no linear front of battle. The battle is ideological and asymmetrical. It is very much a postmodern fight.

We cannot determine the ways in which we fight or the ways in which we must answer in this world—we must act, think and decide as postmodern people. What is so striking is that we are all postmodern whether we "feel" or "think" we are or not. Fundamentally, we must know where we are in our thinking and acting in our lives.

---

[3] Mostly associated with the end of the Second World War, the existential generation. Mostly identified by the popular expression, "live for the moment" because that is all that has meaning for us.

So what if I'm postmodern? Well, the impact seems to be that once I understand this, I can begin to put the larger picture together of who I am, why I make the choices I make, and how I begin to think about the spiritual part of my life in this world. In one sense we have to recover our identity despite the times.

Back on that ridgeline in Afghanistan, all the essential elements came together in one precise time for that young captain and his soldiers. Under fire, they experienced mortality, trust, courage, pain, injury, fear, rising above a situation, hope, and exhilaration. All these things still exist despite a world that seems to be shifting, breaking and changing too fast for us to understand where we are in it. And yet, as it appears to me, you still have the same stuff in you that your grandparents had. You just needed to be put into that ridgeline to see it.

And for many service members, their time in uniform is one of the first times that it all comes together in one place. All those elements of trust, responsibility, courage, discipline, fear, and achievement are daily the stuff of life we encounter. Despite the shifting of any philosophic paradigms, these same elements define you. What you choose to do with them is your call. In those few moments on that ridgeline, your generation rose to the occasion and overcame what appeared to be certain death and annihilation. Shah-I-khot defined your generation as ready to assume all the challenges and responsibilities of this crazy world.

You are made of the right stuff after all.

considerations

Consideration 1: Where does a postmodern person find meaning? Suggestion: You might find meaning hard to define unless you get meaning from your identity in the world. Can all meaning come from my identity? No, maybe some comes from other sources, like your country, your family, your choices. Too, identity meaning helps you because once you know who you are, it is easier for you to help yourself. If knowing yourself gets scary, that is a signal that you may need more help with identity. See a professional who can help and guide you. My generation thought everyone was a kook if they went to a "shrink" but I have come to see more and more that getting help is what it's all about. Seeing a Chaplain is a good start and can often be the place of decision about whether you need more help than conversation. Opening up about yourself and being honest is the starting point. Realize that there is nothing wrong in your asking the hard questions either. Your sense of meaning will grow as you know yourself.

Consideration 2: What makes your thinking different from your parents? Suggestion: If your parents were divorced and remarried and you don't have much to draw from here, perhaps you could think in terms of choices they made and choices you are making now. This is the most powerful thing you can do for yourself—to use your power of choice. Realize that life can be a dirty fight and it is those who pick themselves up from it and begin making right decisions who begin to see success. And it is also critical to remember that all your decisions do not have to be right as long as you learn from the goof-ups!

Consideration 3: If the world is breaking apart, what is the safest thing you could do to protect yourself? Suggestion: Maybe it is a relationship. Maybe it is work. A lot of people find a warm human being is more significant than activities. Just having a friend is pretty important these days. Be careful who you choose to hang out with though and be careful about unfolding your life to a stranger. Let time verify your relationships as genuine. Trust a bit at a time.

ORDER THREE

Believe in God—God has one face and many followers so why is there confusion?

"I'm not aware of too many things,
I know what I know if you know what I mean.
Philosophy is the talk on a cereal box.
Religion is the smile on a dog."

Edie Brickell And The New Bohemians

RELIGION, CULTURE AND BELIEF

I think singer Edie Brickell sums it up for most people because we really don't know what to do with religion. The only time we get religious is at weddings and funerals. Other than that, most people are not waiting in line to get a seat in church on Sunday morning. What Edie suggests is that so much philosophy and religion don't have any relevance to people today though it might have been important at one time. She is satirical, suggesting that both have been "broken down" to things as mundane as cereal box jumble and canine pondering.

I think I've seen my own dog smile on occasion. And I think Edie is right, but why? Because there isn't any set theology anymore. Everybody believes whatever they want. When I talk to most of the soldiers in my division, they are pretty much self-appointed experts in theology. Maybe that is good in a sense because everybody thinks about God or at least religion, of some kind.[4] I will never forget the young soldier in my task force in Somalia sitting on the curb at the Kismayu Airfield smoking a cigarette, wryly smiling and saying to me, "I think I pretty well understand life and religion sir, I think I've got it all figured out." He smiled, self-assured, and outlined to me his concept of life, the world, and his place in it. After I heard it, I knew I had to write a book for these soldiers and for all service members because what he told me I could have learned on a cereal box!

I think one of the foundational things people need to remember about God and how we talk about God, i.e., theology, is that it might appear rather simple but tough minds struggled to make sense of these difficult questions long before you and I ever came along. And their efforts have given me the latitude to shop around and discover all I want about various concepts of God. Without their intense work, we would all still be debating things like nouma, ekklesia, and supralapsarianism.[5] Because they struggled through the difficult questions about sacred scriptures and prophecies I can now discover God for myself not just by my philosophic imagination but by reading theological statements that explain in great detail who God is, and what my place in the world is with respect to God.

A long time ago, theology was made when the experts of the emerging church met together in places like Constantinople or

---

[4] Asking an assorted group of soldiers in a recent breakfast meeting what were the two main issues they dealt with in their lives, 17 percent were concerned about family and relationships and a whopping 22 percent were concerned with religion, then another 16 percent were worried about death and the future. Religion was the big question for most.

[5] You will notice that using complicated terminology helps you see there is a great deal of depth to all studies in theology. However, in this work, it isn't my intention to school you in all these various things but provide you a glimpse of a lead in these footnotes. You learn more about the concepts here in the Greek language when you read a "systematic theology," which sets ideas down in logical sequence with appropriate biblical and philosophic references.

Nicea in the Middle East and hammered out their ideas in the forms of creedal statements. They argued a lot about how they conceived of God and because it was tradition to meet in forums and congresses in order to achieve consensus, they did so. They talked about the amazing things that had happened three hundred years previous to their time and then they sorted out how they could understand God and Jesus Christ and the Holy Spirit. These councils took place in the territory we know today as modern Turkey.[6] Those old guys are dead now but their writings are still on file in libraries—and worth reading too.

Maybe that is what is needed today in order to refocus attention on the ways we talk about God or the ways we can understand God. Sometimes people talk about "reframing" God, and when I say that, I'm referring to the way we picture God to be. That's an odd thing to say, but we are all sort of visual creatures so it is helpful when we can conceive of God as a person like ourselves.

I can't help but wonder what god looks like for many service members because of the current war on terrorism. After all, even the Muslim extremists believe they know and love God, yet why do they want to attack Israeli-based businesses and cause death and maiming in the world? Why does their Jihad allow them the justification to spread terror around the globe? Right now this ought to be a topic of stiff argument in the universities and in the press, but focus is solely on military action. Why aren't young people challenging Muslim Imams about the preaching of hate and the spread of violence? Tough questions ought to be asked about religious intolerance, the essence of true faith, and the ultimate question of what the world looks

---

[6] Air Force personnel are fortunate to be able to be located in places like Incirlik, Turkey, where with some small amount of overland travel they are able to go to these historic sites and actually see the cities and museums where these young guys hammered out the great theological statements that became the basis for both the Eastern Church and the Western Church.

like when any religious extremism is left unchecked. Will there be any tolerance or freedom of religion?

It seems complex but I don't think it is ultimately a very sophisticated or justified position to suggest that Muslim extremists can justify their Jihad. The extremists cloak themselves with a literalistic interpretation of the Koran and believe that a true Muslim goes on Jihad and does that with all his or her might. The French intellectual philosopher Paul Ricoeur[7] made mention years ago in the French journal *L'Esprit*, that the most dangerous aspect of Islam was how it interpreted its scriptures. He made that comment in 1987, now easily seventeen years later it is coming to pass. It is scary when any group becomes ignorantly literalistic. The same goes for religious Christian rightist reconstructionists in America who several years ago sought to kill abortion clinic doctors. Doesn't the Bible say, "Vengence is mine, says the Lord?" What's good for the goose (Muslims) is good for the gander (Christians) as far as I'm concerned. Muslim and Christian alike need to lay down this literalistic crusade and see love and mankind's well-being as the ultimate goal of religion.

For the sailor who may be trudging through this while cramped in his or her bunk at sea, it might help to realize that any religion gone literalistic becomes vicious. I know stories of individuals who stabbed their infant in the crib, and others who put their eyes out because they looked at pornography and believed that God wanted them to do these things in order to be holy. How different is that from this Jihad? None that I can see. Anytime when your religion raises its values above human life it is suspicious. Think before you act. Ask before you dig out those

---

[7] In 1992 I defended my Ph.D. thesis at Protestant Faculty of the University of Strasbourg, France on the topic: "L'idee d'une hermeneutic theologique creatrice selon l'hermeneutic de Paul Ricoeur," 455pp., (Trans: On the concept of a creative theological hermeneutic with reference to Paul Ricoeur's Hermeneutic). Hermeneutics, the science of interpretation, drives politics, beliefs and is the underlying reason for most of the conflict in the world today. But then, who is asking that question?

precious eyeballs because you think this is the biblical requirement for looking at something you think is evil and forbidden.
Ask before you chop off a finger because you used it to steal
something from your shipmate. Your body isn't the evil criminal. Your body simply bears the brunt of a lot of ignorant religious interpretation. It has always been that way in history until
someone figures out that evil is part of the way things are in this
world. Even religion can be evil but that doesn't mean we do
away with it.

So what is the big deal with religion and history anyway?
History seems to be full of examples of where religion caused
death, wars and sorrow. And yet on the other hand religion
played a major part in the development of the American
colonies and the birth of a nation called America. Religion is
like something we can't live with and we can't live without.
America isn't the only religious country in the world either. All
countries and cultures have their religions. Ancestral worship
(China and Southeast Asia), Buddhism and Hinduism (India
and Indonesia), Islam (one of the largest religions in southern
Asia and north Africa), and Christianity are just the big players
of religion in the world. There are over 2500 various religions in
the world today, all of which people claim work, provide meaning for them, and give them a reason to live.

In the service we don't balk at religion at all. It's part of
changes of command, social events, and of course part of the
process of taking care of the dead when they are shipped from
overseas to Dover, Delaware. Who hasn't seen the flag-draped
coffins led by a chaplain on the tarmac? The military admits the
role of religion and has done so for two hundred years of military life. The chaplaincy is the second oldest regiment in the
Army, outranked only by the Engineers. Long before there was
a Navy and Air Force there was an Army with a Chaplain Corps.
And chaplains embody the religious nature of the peoples of the
U.S. wearing uniform and yet belonging to various church and
religious organizations.

But religion holds no surprises for anyone. In fact, religion is boring.

If you think about it, religion is to Christianity what the NFL is to a football team. Nobody really cares about the NFL organization, its functions, its procedures and its organizational charter. But everyone cares about the Super Bowl! And everyone has their favorite teams and players! And that is the way religion ought to be for us too. Religion is only a vehicle for people who like God.

RELIGION IS NOT SPIRITUALITY

Pick a holy man. Most people would quickly say something like "the Dhali Lama." He is a holy man. I agree. The Dhali Lama is a Buddhist monk who gained much notoriety in the late sixties when Beatle John Lennon visited him and wanted to discover his own spirituality in the Far Eastern enclave. Ghandi, Martin Luther (the German guy), and Billy Graham are people we would most quickly associate today with being religious people and holy people I think. However, if religion is the organizational and administrative part, what is this thing called spirituality? Who is spiritual?

Everyone is. That's how we're made. Going back to that concept of the three-part human being, each of us is at the same time body, soul and spirit. It isn't possible to be a human being and not be spiritual. Read me carefully. Spiritual does not mean you are religious and it doesn't mean you chant vespers on your bunk. It means that you are essentially a spiritual creature. That is entirely a different thing. Maybe you have avoided religion for years because you thought you weren't religious enough and in reality, you've been ignoring your essential spirituality all that time!

People in history have always realized they had another part of them that was essentially linked to "something" very different in the world. In some tribal regions, they developed rituals that went along with this suspicion they had and the rituals became their "religion" or their practice of being spiritual. The actual spirituality is something that preceded their religious practices. Often we get things in reverse order and think that rituals will make us spiritual. We are already spiritual. Rituals simply offer our spiritual nature a pathway to God. Just because you may not have related to a ritual that made an impact on your spirituality is not really a reason to stop seeking one that does relate.

We are spiritual human beings because we are made with a sixth sense, so to speak. Our bodies are quite obviously "apparent" and our minds (souls) are always around and we can verify that with our consciences. But our spirits aren't so obvious and in fact they rarely cross our minds. And yet, our spirits and that which defines our spirituality are part and parcel of being a complete human being.

SPIRITUALITY

Nobody wants to be called spiritual. It's like an insult. Why? Probably because spiritual people are no earthly good! That's a well-worn phrase that seems to be true.

I haven't met a spiritual person who didn't also irritate me. I used to be a youth minister in Los Angeles, and had a large volunteer staff that worked with me. One of my volunteers was paid by the church to provide spiritual leadership to the Junior High kids. Whenever I tried to give the guy a list of things to do, he would beam and with a big smile would say, "God Bless you Bill." It was so irritating, I'd tell him to shut up in return. I guess people might have said I wasn't so spiritual. But I think I was. I think the problem with spirituality is that we think that spiritual people are supposed to be retiring, shy individuals who cower to loud noises and mutter religious mantras with their eyes half open. I'm not like that and I don't think being spiritual has anything to do with such a figure.

A spiritual person is in touch with spiritual things. That's it. We're all spiritual human beings but not all of us are in touch with that part of us. We might get close to it once in a while like a friend of mine who entered the Strasbourg Cathedral in France and turned to me in utter amazement and fear and said, "This is a sacred place." Well probably it was a sacred place although I didn't share the emotional punch-in-the-face he did because I'd been in there dozens of times and in many others as well. To me the cathedral was impressive and awe-inspiring but it wasn't necessarily spiritual because it was impressive. But if he made a connection at that point with the cathedral in the sense of his wonder of God and perhaps his smallness in the sight of God (all that said...) then sure, it was a spiritual event for him.

We don't have to try to be spiritual, we are spiritual. We might have to try if we want to "connect" with our spirituality though. We so often fail to realize that our spiritual lives need development just like we'd do physical training in the military, or like we would study in order to go before a military promotion board or train for a special school or course.

During a jungle training exercise with the Infantry, I entered the enemy village after our soldiers had secured the area. The situation was all "make believe" but it was a training event for all of us, to include me, the chaplain. I walked over to where the dead U.S. soldiers had congregated. The guys were all smoking and lying back on their rucksacks, fiddling with their weapons, and talking and laughing as I walked up to their site. I took off my battle gear and my helmet, and donned my black stole. I told them to shut up 'cause they were dead. They laughed and I smiled while ignoring their stares.

As I opened my prayer book and began to speak they got quiet. When I was ready to give burial prayers for each soldier I placed my hand on one soldier's head and prayed, "God bless this soldier and may your peace be upon him from now and into eternity; in the name of the Father, the Son and the Holy Spirit. Amen." As I withdrew my hand his mouth opened and he gazed at his fellow soldiers and then back at me saying, "Sir, I don't know what you did, but when you prayed, something went straight through me!" I turned around to him and said, "No kidding…" The other "dead" soldiers laughed and I continued my rites until all of them had been prayed for. Then I explained more about death and why we took the time to "play this role" for them. It assured the soldiers that in a combat situation they could be assured that in the event of their death the chaplain would find them and pray for them. Someone would be there to honor their spirituality.

As part of the process of praying for those soldiers in the jungle clearing, I also make it my business to read what is indicated on their identification tags, their "dog tags." If a soldier is an atheist I make note of it and move on to the next soldier. While an atheist probably doesn't want a Christian prayer, I do make note that I verified the soldier's religious preference at that time. When the bodies of our fallen service members travel home, the remarks written in a combat theater on those body bags travels home too. That is why it is so important for individuals in the service to note their religious preference on their ID tags so that in the event of their death, they can be assured the type of religious care they wish for their body. Ultimately, it will be someone else who benefits from the thought that a chaplain prayed over your body before it was put into that flag-draped coffin. However, it notes that in all the service branches, chaplains hold to the same conviction, that each soldier is a spiritual person. And each person should take that part of their identity seriously.

Part of the process of going to war involves going through a personnel readiness process. During that time is the best time for sailors, airmen, marines and soldiers to mark their "religious" orientation on their ID tags. If someone puts "no preference" on their tags then prayers will not necessarily be prayed for them in the same manner as they will if it says "Methodist." As a Lutheran minister and chaplain, I respect each service members' convictions and want to insure that even in death people can be confident that their spirituality is respected.

This defines what I'm saying about spirituality the best—we don't put the indicator, "spiritual" on the "dog tags" because that could mean anything and nothing all at once. We put their religion instead. A religious person is not necessarily a spiritual person but a spiritual person can also be a religious person and identify with a tradition. But what are those traditions and why are they important?

RELIGIOUS TRADITIONS

You can be any religion you want, that is your choice. However, you probably will fall into the same thing your parents practiced. I mean it only makes sense that it will happen that way. We tend toward being something quite similar to our upbringing. We don't have to be but it seems that way. Look at it in a different perspective. How many Chinese kids wake up one day and say, "Hey, I'm going to be Southern Baptist!" Highly unlikely isn't it? And so we tend toward something that has the markings of both what we have been raised in and what is similar to our culture.

This might be an uphill discussion for many of you but it is critical in trying to understand the "why" of religions. I will oversimplify the discussion but it might be new to most who read this. Though all religions are based usually on an individual's teachings, holy or sacred documents or sacred ideas and concepts passed down from one generation to another, all religions are also based upon several non-sacred things that tend to govern their power in a people and in the world:

+ Cultural uniqueness of a society.
+ Perceptions of the world and how that world ends.
+ How we know what we know (epistemology).

Again, I will make this as simple as possible. Each of these is a huge discussion, but we don't have the time and space to entertain them at that length. If you want to know more just look in the footnotes and you can go wild on your research.[8] I want to give you an overview of each of these so that you can understand the function of religion. Notice, I'm not saying which religion, just religion itself. It will be your decision as to whether you want to be religious as a Catholic, a Buddhist, or a Methodist.

My experience is that most people who claim to be religious have little idea that most of their religious orientation has been donated to them by family, culture and mythic orientations and less by choice, preference and convenience. However, if you take a few minutes to discover how religion is put together you might understand the tattoos on your lower back!

CULTURE AND RELIGION

The place we grow up, the economics, the traditions and the way people express themselves have everything to do with how we interpret God and express God in terms of religion and religious traditions.

In Central America the Mayan Indians' empire dissolved and was replaced with the colonial discoverers' religion of Catholicism. In the current Central American region, Catholicism still holds sway over the teeming poor cities and jungles spawned by a concept of liberation from economic oppression tied to redemption. Liberation theology, as it is known by the Catholic church, is the meat and potatoes religion of the peoples of Central America. Yet Catholicism is also in Germany but not as "liberation theology" but as a leftover from the crisis of the Protestant Reformation in the 1500s. The German nobility liked the idea of the Reformation and embraced Martin Luther's Reformation ideas because they freed

---

[8] Read Joseph Campbell's works on Religion and Culture; Mircea Eliade, *The Myth of the Eternal Return*; Paul Ricoeur, *Symbolism of Evil* and *Time and Narrative*; Rheinhold Niebuhr, *Christ and Culture*.

the nobles from the excessive taxes of the Roman Catholic church and empowered the individual worker to own property, produce and sell products. Once freed from the oppressive taxation Germany's economy surged, not based on Catholic liberation but based on being liberated from Catholicism and its control on economic production in Germany. In this example we see how culture holds sway over both types of societies. In each place, Central America and Germany, there are different ways of experiencing the same catholic religion however very differently.

Culture shapes its religion to conform with the way of life of a people so that it is "seamless" so to speak. In China, the state and Mao are the religious orientation of a billion people. They don't have freedom of speech and so their religion conforms to such restrictions. The ancestral worship of the Chinese conforms to a non-threatening "religious" part of the Chinese state and philosophy. Mao's sayings are both the mantra and the glue

which holds together a nation of people who find "god" within rather than outside of themselves.

African tribes are animistic and hold to mythic suspicions about God. God is in the sky, the shrubs, the animals and these things hold certain power over individuals. However, the African culture is variegated. In south Africa, European Dutch Reformed theology still has quite a hold in the religious thinking of South Africans due to the Dutch settlers of the nineteenth century. Throughout Africa you will find a vast divergence of religion based on colonization and its effects on the particular nations and with its juxtaposition to tribal animism.

Even in America, our culture differs from state to state and region to region so that a white person from New England is nothing like a white person from San Francisco and a black in the back woods of Georgia is vastly different than a black person from Seattle. Religious practice differs and theological understanding is influenced by traditions, history, local suspicions and by who is the most powerful in a town or state. Our own Civil War had much to do with biblical interpretation of the right to own slaves, a position not necessarily unbiblical in the history of ancient biblical tradition.[9]

Economics influence our belief. People in a technological society don't give in easily to ideas of God in the trees. People in the tribal areas of Irian Jaya don't readily accept the idea of getting into an elevator for fear of their being buried alive in a box. Money alters our sense of security and often takes away our sense of the need for the divine. Disease can either be something we treat or the scourge of God. All of these particulars influence our religious orientation. This is one of the central reasons why there are so many kinds of denominations of Christian faith for example. It doesn't mean they are either all wrong or all right. They are all somewhat different, shaped by culture.

I have conducted a couple of retreats with soldiers from the former DDR or East German Army. All of the soldiers come from a simple country town west of Berlin where they grew up during the communist regime from 1945 until 1989. Due to the fact that Christian ideas were outlawed during that time and that allegiance to state policies was the law of the land, these young soldiers have no concept of God at all. The Bible makes no sense to them because they have no concept of a loving God

---

[9] Philemon is a very small book in the Bible in which the Apostle Paul counsels a young businessman to take good care of his slave. In the book of Romans, the same Apostle Paul never speaks out against slavery. However, Paul would have condemned the ill-use and beating of slaves to accomplish an economic objective. Some of those colonialist slave owners obviously contorted scripture to justify their hate and abuse of black human beings. However, there are moving stories of compassionate slave owners. One black Chaplain acquaintance of mine from South Carolina kept the name "Collecton" which was the name of the slave owner of his family because of their deep love and admiration for his Christian compassion to Grandparents in the 1800s. There are good stories!

who might have worked as a creator and sustainer of life in the world and also possesses a love and concern for them. Since all their lives the state has provided their existence, there is no God for them. This illustrates how our concepts of God are determined in large measure by our environments, our economies and our traditions. However, it is also important to make note that the director of these retreats is also a former East German who grew up in the same system and yet whose family held a firm belief in God. She and her family decided to maintain their belief in God despite the overwhelming punishment that went along with professing faith in a god other than the communist state![10] This story can be repeated over and over again in Germany.

Our concepts of God are often not necessarily correct though they may be popular.

PERCEIVING THE END OF THE WORLD

I know this sounds like a doomsday philosophy but it is a simple rule: Determine what the end looks like and I can tell you what you believe. In theology it is called eschatology. Eschatology is the study of the "end things."

How the world ends determines how we live and react in our world. In regions of the world where cultures believe in reincarnation, people hope to come back in a next life as something of a higher life-form with a better position in life. Where people believe in resurrection, they hope, like in Israel. They hope for a brighter future and to lose hope is the greatest sin. Always hope for a better future because there will be a new day. Christians,

---

[10] Heidi Brauer and her husband Bernd are an amazing story of courage in the face of government opposition. As an adult, Bernd worked on a project in East Germany developing LED crystals, which we find commonplace in our techno toys today. Bernd invented LEDs but his files were taken by his government supervisor as his own and Bernd was deprived of his invention rights. Bernd is retired today and Heidi works for the Evangelishes Militaar-pfarrer's office in Berlin forming retreats to introduce soldiers to the good news of the Gospel.

most of the people who read this, believe that not only will there be a resurrection, there will also be a new heaven and a new earth, no more tears. These ideas of how the world ends determine how people read their sacred books or documents and how and why they practice or don't practice their religion.

The Apostle Paul says in Corinthians that if in this life we have hoped only in Christ that this hope is sufficient for us because of the quality of the life. For Paul he believed in resurrection and that if we gave our lives for Christ and his sake that we would be rewarded in heaven. And so, it was easier for Christians to go into the coliseum and be burned alive or eaten by animals. When one martyr was being burned at the stake it is reported that he saw Christ welcoming him into eternal bliss.[11] With that sort of hope "at stake" it was easier for people to face persecution.

By viewing the end we can understand why Baptists believe that it is important to be saved today, because Christ will return visibly in the sky soon, there will be a great battle, the devil will be defeated and we will all live in a kingdom where Jesus sits on a throne. Some Baptists and Methodists, and varieties of them all, also hold that Jesus will come and retrieve all the Christians and that the battle will take place without us. Others, like the Lutherans, believe that Christ has come again and that we are shaping the kingdom into existence right now. Others like some Reformed churches, Presbyterians and Evangelicals, believe that we must go through the time of tribulation, fight and then Christ will come again to save us.

On the other side, militant extremist Muslims believe that they are on a crusade to annihilate evil and establish God's rule on earth. Muslims, Jews and Christians are "aggressor" religions for lack of a better term because they are founded on the kingdom concept. Kingdoms imply kings, and kings usually take control in a battle. Muslim Jihad is interpreted violently at

---

[11] You have to read *Foxe's Book of Martyrs*, a classic that tells all these tales in easy to read English.

present. Jews hope and wait for Messiah who will establish his kingdom in Jerusalem and rule. Christians hope for salvation from above in Christ the King. And where the end involves only death and return to ashes, there is little need for violent struggle, and there is evident lack of interest in the temporal life as in India where the masses hope for a better tomorrow through rebirth.

So you see, the way you view the "end of the matter" in your religion will determine your present practice of religious faith. Eschatology also influences your view of material possessions and relationships. Christians in America are always working, striving and hoping for a better day. That day is material, physical, emotional, governmental, or whatever. It is better. We believe in a progressive concept of our economy because our faith is forward looking. We essentially believe that things can get better. However, because we view things this way we aren't necessarily too focused on the quality of our lives internally—we are mostly focused on things outside us. In the Far East, the inner quality is much more important than outward quality. I think this is one reason Americans are always fascinated with Mother Theresas and Dhali Lamas, because in the simplicity of their lives they offer something more substantial than fast cars, good-looking women, big condos, and lots of money.

In an interesting turn of events in Somalia I learned quite a bit about the value of things and human life when a young father determined to run a checkpoint where some of my battalion's soldiers were holding guard. When he failed to stop his vehicle, the soldiers opened fire, sending the man and his truck careening into the ditch. Holes peppered the side of the Nissan truck. The driver dismounted and began screaming in anger at the American soldiers who had destroyed his truck in the hail of bullets. Remarkably the man survived with only wounds as he asked for payment for his truck. A young GI called his sergeant over and said, "Hey Sarge, come here and look." As the sergeant looked in the back of the pickup there were two small children riddled with bullets. The young soldier turned in disbelief and threw up in the street. The father turned when questioned about the payments and said that he could easily get two more boys but he couldn't get a new truck.

What we believe determines how we value things. If the end is more important than the present, we might forfeit anything to achieve it. Jim Jones bluffed nine hundred followers with the same eschatological fantasy in Guyana twenty years ago. They drank Kool-aid laced with cyanide because they believed in something in the future they could only reach through death.

It will always be true too that you can measure the goodness of a religion by its end state. It must make sense, and it cannot violate human beings' essential human rights. I think there are good parts to all religions, but not all religions seek your best interest. Right now, we are seeing the worst display of Muslim theology as typified in the Taliban and Al Qaeda interpretation. I often ask myself what is their end-state? How do they view things when all evil Westerners are obliterated? And I also ask how that is justifiable? But too, we must ask this question of our religion and its ultimate end. All of these things are governed by the way we validate truth.

HOW WE KNOW WHAT WE KNOW (EPISTEMOLOGY)

One more time a hard word, epistemology. The way we determine or come up with our idea of truth. This one concept could take a discussion of a thousand pages. I don't have that much room to write. I will put it rather succinctly if I can. The way we know how we believe is the great war of religions.

Back to the soldier on the sidewalk in Kismayu. I don't know how that young medic determined how he knew all the things he did about life and the world. But I do know this, his method of determining that was the single most powerful influence in his life. I find that most service members are pretty confident about their epistemologies! There is something about military life and the rough and tumble association most find themselves thrust into that urges them to quickly determine their truth indicator.

Epistemology is our way of knowing. I call it a truth indicator. In other words, when I speak to soldiers I realize that depending on their truth indicator, they will either turn me off or they'll listen. If someone is an atheist, they believe that God doesn't exist. However, that becomes their epistemology too. Your truth indicator is like a formula. Once you enter certain assumptions, the calculator starts flashing. Belief in God is a foundational factor. Once you do away with God as a given truth, all other things immediately are affected by that. For instance, once God does not exist you suddenly have no reference to greatness outside of yourself, and no "revelation" outside of yourself. The greatest thing in life suddenly becomes something or someone else, like yourself perhaps. Because I do not exist then I can't be around to experience other things.

Believing in God references greatness beyond me and immediately suggests that there are things greater and perhaps more interesting than the limited world I can see and experience. Believing in God suggests that there are many things I may need to discover about that God. It may also suggest that the God I believe in is distinctly different than your God, as in the Somali father versus the American soldiers' concept of God.

The process of how I know God exists is the process of epistemology. I can't undertake to explain much more about this here but it is sufficient to realize that this is the way religion is put together. Epistemology is the reason there are essential and critical differences between Shintoism and Methodism, between Reincarnation and Justification by Faith. Yet few young people take the time to realize this powerful tool of the truth indicator.

Most of the soldiers I run into day by day sort of bob along on the sea of ideas and are completely unaware of the power of how we know truth and how we determine truth factors (truth coherence, we call it in philosophy). I once studied under a brilliant and curious individual named Dr. John Warwick Montgomery who suggested that the danger of not understanding truth theory leaves me helpless to defend the statement someone might suggest that "there is a little Man in the Moon who makes cheese." Unless I believe in a one-to-one truth theory I cannot refute the statement about the Man in the Moon.[12] When our concept of how we know things is based merely on our own whimsical opinions and we are comfortable with that, everything else in our life will fall into little categories based on those opinions.

And if my way of knowing truth is the only way of knowing truth, then I will forever be my own authority on life, the world and faith. However, if I have the least bit of suspicion that perhaps there is more for me to discover about truth and myself, then perhaps I should open myself up to the discovery of what religion and spirituality is all about and where I fit with respect to it.

Confusion over God, religion and spirituality exists. It seems to only clear up as individuals seek God. Seeking God seems to be the one sure way to initiate your spirituality in a serious way. Others simply sit on the curb believing their

---

[12] Coherence theory of truth. One-to-one suggests that things are evident and measurable; i.e., man is human and to be human is to be mortal, and to be mortal is to eventually die. All this is one-to-one. But if I say that man is human and to be human is to live forever, then suddenly I have exploded the equation. How do I get to this foreverness? How did I cease being a dying human? Truth-coherence theory is especially important in the way we measure how we talk about reality.

minds are clear, ignorant of all the great minds and hard work that have gone before them, and suggest they have the answers to life they might have gleaned from a cereal box.

considerations

Consideration 1: Considered studying the history of ideas? There are as many ideas in history as there are people to provide them. One of the most productive things you can do is study the core ideas of history. There is a set of five paperback books entitled, *The Encyclopedia of the History of Ideas* (and others if that is out of print) which detail all the major ideas of history and provides you with additional reading to understand them. It isn't easy going and could help you go to sleep at night as well! How can understanding ideas help you develop your intellectual faith?

Consideration 2: Is there one right religion? I guess as a Christian I should say yes. I would say that out of my study of the history of ideas, of theology and of my understanding of my epistemology for Christian faith. However, I'm also open-minded enough to suggest that I think there are variations on "right." It isn't possible intellectually for Christians to allow for other "right" answers, and that is a problem if we are trying to be politically correct. However, I do think intellectually it is possible. So, for my personal faith, I subscribe to a Christian faith based upon the Bible's truth statements. But for my intellectuality, which God has given us all too, I believe there may be alternative and right pathways for people to believe in God. Like the Apostle Paul said on Mars Hill (cited in the book of Acts) there were altars to the unknown gods to which Paul admitted that people sought

God the best they could. Even though I think my way may be epistemologically correct, I think there may be other ways to God that are as correct as a people may be able to conceive of due to their cultural orientation. What are the critical elements to religion for you? Ultimately it is your answer to this question that means more than whether you can answer it for everyone else. As a Christian, I also know that my theology says that we will all be judged by the amount of light that we each have.

Consideration 3: How do you understand the end of all things? Let's think for a minute that it does matter in order to answer this. Can you state how things end for the world as we know it (to quote REM). If so, then how do you make that assumption about the end? Where does it begin for you? Upon what do you base that start point? Determine your truth-coherence factor so you know what and how you make those big statements about reality.

ORDER FOUR

Understand Your Faith—Ask yourself the right questions before you assert your opinion about ultimate truths.

"the only dumb question is the one which is not asked..."

unknown

THE BEST ANSWER BEGINS WITH THE RIGHT QUESTION

This book is about the answers. Everyone wants them or at least wants people to think they have them already. But all answers begin with questions. And the best answers are found when the right questions are asked. If you sidestep the questioning process, the answers you have already developed may give way when the tough times come. Better to have asked before you answer and don't know what the question ever was.

I want you to think "way outside the wire" in this chapter. Try for a minute to suspend all the things you've been taught and go back to the fundamental assumptions of the way you formulate your belief system. Though we will talk about belief systems later, here I want you to begin questioning your faith—in a good sense. Years ago when I went to Strasbourg, France, to study and work on my doctorate, this well-meaning person told me to watch out for those professors at the university lest I earn my doctorate and lose my faith at the same time. I thought that was a curious way to approach thinking. It is a fearful way to think. It doesn't have to be a threatening process. Questions don't have to dislodge the faith you have unless maybe you're already uncertain about your allegiance to your own self. And that's where being honest with yourself (Order One) comes into being an important first step for understanding your faith.

One of the most difficult things for us to do is to trust our own mind. Yet from my perspective, if I am a God-designed human being and every part of me is sacred, then my thinking, is probably sacred too. Sacred in the sense that there is nothing wrong with thinking even though at times my thinking might take me way far away from what is "normative" and sacred in the sense of being morally "correct" for ourselves. But our intellects themselves are as sacred as our bodies are. The soldiers who saw the kids in the back of the pickup truck in Somalia were aghast that human life was so cheap to the Somali father. Part of that sense is that human life in the West is considered God-given, another way of saying it is sacred. It's not just our bodies I believe God has made sacred, it is also our thinking processes. Everything is sacred and created by God and good.

In this chapter I travel outside the lines of economics, race and religion to a place where we can talk about the way we think. My assumption is that most all of us wade into our points of view about God, reality, life and our ultimate concerns, without ever asking the question of how we came to think about those things.

One of the most obvious qualities about the current postmodern philosophy is that people who are postmodern usually do not trace their thinking process backwards to discover how in the world they got where they did—they just assess things which are at close reach to them and leave "cause and effect" alone. And yet, that was Jenny's problem in not making the connection with her past. And people choose not to make connections for various reasons. Maybe the past is painful, or maybe they don't see any relevance in it at first look, or perhaps they figure they made their choices with the best capability they had at the time and they're not going to retrace their steps. "To hell with it," in other words. OK, but if that is where you end up then you wouldn't be reading this would you?

It is just as annoying to hear a preacher go on and on about all the things you "ought" to be doing and which you do not feel you can accomplish to be "holy" as it is to hear a conversation where one sailor talks to another and espouses his or her philosophy about life and reality as if they had just received a transmission from God alone. You will find this book doesn't "preach" to you but challenges you to do the mental work to bring your thinking into perspective and see if it meets with some of the common sense tests that make your opinion about life, ultimate truth and/or God, valid or not.

So, let's see if in this order, there is something to learn about our thinking that will move us from where we are to a place of better understanding about ultimate things. Measure your thinking as you go along.

BARRACKS LAWYERS, DOCTORS AND MINISTERS

This is the affectionate term for what is done everywhere in the service by well-meaning service members who attempt to manage their lives with "inside" help from other service members who seem to "know" stuff that will help them figure out a problem without having to get professional help. It's not so time consuming and the chain of command doesn't have to find out anything about them. Problem is that the information often dispensed in a hundred barracks and ships around this globe doesn't come with much of a guarantee. And the results often are lopsided and end up causing more problems than the information is worth. Hopefully, this chapter will help you with issues that come from my area of expertise—religion, and the way you develop your faith in this world. It comes with the guarantee that once you've worked your way through this part of the book you will be able to articulate your issues about ultimate issues like god, faith and belief in a god, and know where you are in the process. It is my conviction that it is as important to know where you are in the process as it is where you end up.

I'm not suggesting that you will turn into a religious person by thinking real hard about God every day. I am convinced though that if you start thinking about how you got where you are today, that this will furnish you with a sense of where God is for you today. I define this as a four-step process that involves asking the right Questions, discovery of your philosophic and religious Orientation, development of personal Convictions and the making of courageous Choices which correspond to the other three.

One word of caution for you: Order Four is a take-off point, i.e., you probably cannot get through this chapter without some sort of personal departure in terms of your personal life and faith. I don't suggest that you will become a Christian as a result of this but you will define yourself so that by the time you work through these four elements, you will ask some tough questions that will have the effect of getting you "calibrated" as a machinist might say. It is my opinion that even Christian faith requires some tough thinking. I say this because of the groundless allegation that somehow Christian theology is easy to assimilate whereas Eastern religions are more complex and somehow much more "durable." I disagree. I think all religions have their complex dimensions. Christian faith happens to be the predominant faith of many Americans and Europeans, yet this doesn't mean it is as easy as going to the base exchange! Yet many service members treat Christian faith as a sort of beginners' religion and often branch off into Eastern religion or even sectarian philosophies like Dianetics and Scientology because these offer a more complex and interesting journey. From my perspective, a faith that can enable people to endure animal goring, crucifixion and being burned alive before a crowd of roaring Roman citizens, and still survive two thousand years with hardly a change in story certainly is toe-to-toe as strong a religion as eastern Hindu mysticism. Sometimes I think Westerners are romanced by the East. See Order Three about Religion for more.

Asking the Right Questions

There is no incorrect question. But there is also no forbidden question. The forbidden questions draw our attention more than the incorrect questions. Incorrect is an assessment put on our questions by teachers and supervisors. Forbidden is a moral assessment we put on questions ourselves. These days incorrect questions are only for work, not for life. Forbidden questions have everything to do with our lives and the results of so many things which are happening to us.

Most of my counseling with soldiers is like this. Most people who talk with me about their problems tell me about two parts of the problem. One part is the military unit's issue with them (the correct and incorrect stuff) and the other part is the personal effect of their situation (the forbidden questions). And how things affect "us" is way more important than how or what the unit is going to do with us or to us. I find most of you who read this are very interested in yourselves. For whatever reason, today's service members can face some terrific adjudication by their units but when it comes to their personal feelings, perspectives and relationships, these things are the most important of all. Many times, forbidden things have interrupted their life. And many of these stories enter my office for help.

One of the most frustrating parts about being a military chaplain is that by the time you get to me, your world is crashing in around you. If you had just taken the time to work yourself through a process like this right now, you'd avoid a great deal of pain. So, let's go.

What are the forbidden questions you have? Most of your forbidden questions probably have to do with situations or results which involved a moral lapse or failure. Often people ask the moral questions when they are aware that the situation has risen to a point where it seems the most pressing questions are the embarrassing ones. And the embarrassing questions are moral ones. We become embarrassed because moral, failures involve the "cause and effect" breakdown between our choices and other real people. When we fail and that failure involves a person, the failure becomes moral and the questions surrounding that event or breakdown are forbidden. These are the questions about whether I should abort the child I'm carrying, or whether I should tell anyone that so and so was sleeping on shift, or sleeping with my friend, or whether anyone will notice the cash missing from the safe. Morals always have to do with our relationship with people.

But these moral questions, why would they be an issue? Forbidden questions arise because somewhere a person has failed to identify where they come from morally. And they may never have taken the time to ask tough questions about the beliefs they have. So even though in their "hearts" they may feel disoriented or confused about circumstances, their questions about morals are not even the most important at this point. The best question to ask is why?

Why do I hold to any of the moral feelings I do? And why does it ultimately matter? Why can't everyone just be who they are and work things out? Well, the world isn't put together in a "random" sort of process. There is an order, and some things are always going to be right and other things always wrong. For instance, it is always right to be kind to others. It is always wrong to keep your kids locked in a car in the middle of summer with the windows rolled up while you shop at Wal-Mart for an hour. Why is it always this way? Because of the rule of "cause and effect." This is too easy to figure. It is always going to be that there are rights and wrongs. Yet, today, these are blurring so that one of the reasons service members have so many forbidden-issue questions is due to this blurring.

And how does the blurring occur? By our failure to understand this world of rights and wrongs and causes and effects. Right and wrong have become negotiable. But that is an oxymoron. Right ought to be always right and wrong ought to be always wrong if a community wishes to be able to function. Imagine a football game where the players were allowed the freedom to blur the yardage and call a "first down" when the ten-yard line was still five yards away. Imagine the referee only suggesting that this could be wrong but that due to the feelings of the players and because of his own preferences that this was really right?! Football doesn't work that way, nor does any other game. Rules determine the correspondence between what is right and wrong without which nothing would make sense at all and no one could function.

The American individualism under which most of our youth have grown up has infected our moral consciences so that it is very common today for me to speak to people who have a negotiated moral balance so that it weighs in their favor regardless of what anyone thinks. And how do people get to this point? By not understanding the sense of the need for balance. Disregarding the metaphor of the game, most young people entering the service today have to learn their service branch's "values" in order to function on the military team. It use to be that these things were assumptions where we all grew up. But no longer. Now, nobody can take for granted that you understand the same values I understand.

Further, it seems too that what I call the "god index" is missing. The East German soldiers I worked with did not put god into their intellectual thinking process, and so they were missing the moral aspect of their questions and only asked for correct or incorrect answers. Right is either correct or incorrect. And if it has been determined for me that something is not correct, then it is not right. But this lack of moral aspect doesn't include a "god index." When the concept of God cannot be included in someone's thinking, they tend towards simply being correct or incorrect. And yet the world is much bigger than simply being right or wrong because of statistics or usefulness.

You have to ask yourself where the "god index" is for yourself. This is where questions start to be a bit more forbidden because these questions start to open up the issue of a moral God who has input into your personal life. And you cannot talk about God without talking about people. Jewish tradition believes that your relationship with God has everything to do with how you treat people. In this sense, when we talk about God we start getting close to "forbidden" type questions.

For example, how did your parents fit God into your thinking process when you were little? How were things understood in your life when for instance a loved one died? Was the word "god" simply a profanity or was god an individual or object of worship you tried to know? I tried to make this understandable to my kids when they were very little by illustrating how God interacted with our family and their lives. I knew things were looking up when on a camping trip my oldest son, then two years old, followed me to a mountain lake and uttered the remarkably clear theological statement, "…lake, God made." Though that connection may seem simplistic, for him the connection was clear because I had made it clear to him when he was a child. Since kids are naïve, they accept what they are taught to believe. Today as a Marine Lieutenant, he still believes God made the lakes and the human beings over which he has care, duty and command.

What was built into your thinking process at an early age is probably part of the thinking process you have today and drives your questions.

There shouldn't be forbidden questions about God. In fact it is healthy to question God, his existence, his role in the world, and the problem of whether God answers prayer.[13] During exceptionally troubling times I have often spoken my mind with God. At one time I was being told to leave a church in Chicago and I felt I had failed the people and failed God (though there was no reason for either). Yet I became really upset about the entire thing and questioned God ruthlessly. On another occasion in the military, I could not understand how I could hold up working for a particular boss and I seemed to always be in emotional knots going to work. "Where was God when I needed him?" seems to be the most prayed prayer I know of.

We need to be able to separate the difference between our understanding of God and God's understanding of us. It might do us good to assume the best about God despite our inability to perceive of God "correctly," i.e., in an orthodox way.

Theologically, God doesn't discriminate against you because you've never prayed, or because since joining the service you never go to chapel, or because you've fallen into some moral failure from which you see no exit. This is the great thing about understanding God from the Bible. As a theologian, I know for certain that the history and reputation God has indicates that whenever you are capable of asking the hard questions, God is capable of bringing some light and answers to you.

Yet you have to ask the questions. You cannot be afraid of being a skeptic. Bring your skepticism to God openly. There is no set format for praying to God about anything. You've probably heard "the Lord's Prayer" spoken at a funeral or on television, but that format isn't the only way to pray. Sometimes just getting alone and talking works best, or writing your feelings down in a journal, or taking a walk and simply thinking toward

---

[13] If you don't question God with tough questions you can't get good answers! Look at some tough questions in the book *Mere Christianity*, by C.S. Lewis or some interesting perspectives about God in *Your God Is Too Small* by J.B. Philips, or see some challenging ideas in *Escape from Reason* by Francis A. Schaeffer.

God. Whatever format you chose, do something which initiates this encounter with God and brings your questioning to God.

What about Right Questions though? The right questions are the honest questions. Questions posed with an honest heart, whether they challenge core beliefs or not, are good questions to ask. Questions like this reveal a person is truly seeking an answer, possibly truly seeking God.

So you see, there are not "right" questions necessarily, but just honest ones. Our problem is we attempt to lie to whoever we think God is and figure that that process is supposed to be spiritual or effective when in reality it is just mindless babble. First we must be honest with ourselves. We must look back into our family, our lives, and determine where the "god index" is. Then we must ask honest questions like:

Do I believe in God?

Can I trust a God who says he loves me?

Where has God touched my life before?

Why don't I feel like God is near me?

How can I believe in a God who allows evil?

Why do my emotions conflict with my belief about God?

What should I believe and what form should that take?

As long as you are in the question mode, you can't go wrong. I would rather that every service member asks these sorts of questions than the forbidden questions because if they answer any of these they will begin healing themselves by virtue of the powerful effect the answer to any of these questions can bring.

"What should I believe?" is a great starting question. Is there a "correct" or "right" answer to this? No, not necessarily. Essentially, it is important for you to believe in a god at least because the concept of a god in the universe brings to each of us a sense that life is bigger than ourselves, our country, our issues. And if we can get to that point then perhaps if that God cares about human beings he also cares about you and me. Now once

I get that far, I am very close to understanding the Christian sense of a creator-god who loves individuals and wants their best. However, that is my Christian Orientation. We will talk more about Orientation in a moment.

Questions are sacred in my understanding. If you take away that one fact, you are way ahead in understanding the importance of our minds when it comes to ultimate things. Ask the hard questions, and keep a notebook of them. Seek the best answers that seem to make sense all the way around. Don't simply dictate what your family said to you but think through what you do know. That means we have to talk about Orientation.

DISCOVER YOUR ORIENTATION

Everybody is different. Despite these differences, few take time to orient themselves culturally, philosophically or religiously.

One of the scariest parts of being in the Army is facing a Land Navigation Course at night. Each soldier is teamed up with another, given a map, a compass and a requirement to get from points A to Z within so much allotted time. Many teams end up frustrated and lost. Teams arrive at the finish line with bruises, scrapes and stories of being disoriented until  they came upon some piece of terrain they recognized or some compass heading that finally put them in the right direction. I find many military guys and girls are sort of lost on their navigation through life because they can't get oriented.

I met such a sergeant one afternoon while casually waiting for another staff meeting—she was an intelligent flight medic, about twenty-five years old, a very engaging personality and attractive. For some reason we exchanged glances and began some small talk. The question I asked her, very common for any of us in the military, was, "Where are you from?" The answer was complex. Her life had been a remarkable and sometimes nearly disastrous journey. Her mother had remarried a religious man who decided the family would move to a commune. They all moved into the commune, and she and her sister began to realize that part of the regime of the commune was a blurring of social lines. The leader of the commune was allowed to sleep with any of the females in the society. As the sergeant described the story she seemed okay and continued on to tell how she personally felt this was wrong and convinced her sister to escape with her. Her parents would not support her conviction that anything in the commune was wrong. She escaped to a grandparent's location, finished high school, entered the Army and became a flight medic. That afternoon, in between staff meetings, I asked her if she still believed in God. She replied, "Yes I do. I never let what I experienced determine how I understood God. I believe in God and know that God was watching over me and my sister the entire time." She had survived an incredible journey, oriented herself, and continued on with her life putting little things into place bit by bit until she made sense of it all. She made getting herself oriented and on the right track a priority and it paid off.

Getting oriented is tough and even tougher in situations like that. When individuals get disoriented spiritually, they tend to drift aimlessly in life, pinging off of people and events without much direction. Sometimes even religion takes them to situations where they never can trust again as in this sergeant's life. When that occurs they often never return to religion, god or faith. They assume no one who practices religion can be trusted and they are "lost" on the sea of life. They tie up to wherever makes sense to them. Yet, this missing element of what is their ultimate purpose in life also tends to drift unanswered. Unless a person is exceptional, they can't answer these questions without some help. And sooner or later life has a way of shooting a torpedo into our hull and sinking our opinions just when we need them most.

Not everyone can survive like the young Non-Commissioned Officer (NCO) I met in Hawaii that day. Many simply never get oriented and never recover. It doesn't always take a bizarre situation to dislodge people. I've seen individuals from all economic levels and situations fail to get situated philosophically and religiously, ending up wandering in institutions like our military. Just when you need that inner source of clarity and direction, it fails to surface, and when you could have made a difference for your team, you fail.

Orienting is facing the hard questions about where you come from and sorting out where you are in reference to them. This is part a philosophic process and part religious.

This is made harder today due to our individualism. We are all heavily influenced by a techno-heavy society with constant appeals to our individual satisfaction. Most American service members are luckier than their peers in the U.S. because their travels take them outside of this excessively individualistic culture to countries where they see the "other side" of the world. Airmen who have the opportunity to get off Base in Central America will see the kids who sniff paints and glues and die in the sewer in Honduras. Sailors going ashore in Italy and Spain will see the transients from North Africa begging for asylum with the Port Police. Many of these die from exposure and drowning in the Mediterranean just like they do coming from Cuba today. We just don't hear about it in the U.S. Soldiers in Germany see the undesirable Turkish and Gypsies camped out along the roads and fields. There are other cultures with their unlovely cultural "parasites" as well as their individualistic western converts too. Large expensive automobiles and motorcycles. Service members deployed to

Afghanistan see opportunist Muslims there as much as they do in Bosnia and Kosovo. People tend to ignore where they are in light of their current satisfaction. Seeing this is helpful. Perhaps it can help you to start asking yourself the right questions about life and spirituality instead of just pursuing your own narcissistic desires.

Everyone who might develop a spiritual orientation from the rich European culture does not necessarily do so. Proximity to greatness does not necessarily drift into people's hearts and minds. The land of the Enlightenment and Reformation provide no more a beneficial influence to Europeans than does the U.S., the land of the Constitution and Bill of Rights yield goodness and philanthropy to Americans. Just showing up in your culture doesn't mean you know where you are within it.

We need to understand our philosophic orientation in terms of what is important to us. What are the things I place value in? These come about in direct proportion to my culture and my upbringing. They also develop as a result of my needs. In a society as well-fed and cared for as Europe and America, most young people have needs at a very high level of gratification in contrast to primal needs like shelter and food. Depending on where you are in the world your needs will be determined by an economic hierarchy of needs.

So where are you in that hierarchy? You can quickly determine this by asking yourself which of the previous questions have any relevance to you. As a rule, we do not ask "metaphysical" questions (i.e., questions about God, existence, ultimate truths…) while we are occupied with a Sony PlayStation. It just isn't as important to us. Yet, when we are taken from that level and put into a infantry platoon searching a village in Afghanistan and a grenade explodes in the jeep we're driving, suddenly survivability, fear and faith become more vivid. I'm sure the sailors on the USS *Cole* thought long and hard about ultimate questions after the fire died out in that harbor in

Yemen a few years ago. Once again, being military has its advantages for helping you understand some of the most important things in life.

Your philosophy may not be articulated in a sophisticated way, but you do need to understand certain things about whether God exists, whether human beings have human rights, whether it matters if we have values. If you and I cannot answer this sort of question then perhaps we haven't gotten oriented yet. It is one thing to be able to yell out your service motto, another to be able to live that motto. If you are orienting, then you should be able to make a connection with where you've come from, your culture, your beliefs, and your values, and where you are today.

You may not embrace your service values in your heart though you might say them when you have a formation as a unit. However, to own up to where you have come from is the best start. The young flight medic knew where she had come from, she knew how it was abnormal and she was putting herself into the correct alignment with a new set of values that she could personally embrace.

Figure that your culture will involve your religious background, your ethnicity and the things which are important models or images for you. For some this might be things like possessions—cars, play toys like boats and motorcycles, or just money. For others it might be volunteering with scouts or starting a small business. And others might value popularity, or power—sometimes women find themselves thirsting for leveraged power whereas men want brute power and so they go for "He-man" type professions in the military (Rangers, Special Forces, SEALs etc).

Ethnicity plays into orientation heavily due to the fact that many groups of service people tend to flock in groups that are divided according to color. Hispanics, Blacks and Whites are still divided in their interests but often this becomes a division of power rather than simply one of convenience. Some use their orientation to wield power over others and fall into typical racial stereotype roles. Not thinking about our abusive ethnic orientation often cripples harmony aboard a ship and divides platoons, making cohesion impossible.

There are subgroups of all of these ethnic divisions too. White "former gang/skin heads" can ostracize suspected homosexual service members and threaten them, sometimes leading to homocide or suicide. A young black soldier may be influenced to become a Mason and then kept out of the power and influence if he decides to abstain from becoming one. An Hispanic enlisted female may be expected to submit to a traditional social hierarchy of male submission when approached by an errant NCO to provide sexual favors. White females from both lower class and upscale backgrounds may find sexual gratification is also a tool for workplace favors and gains

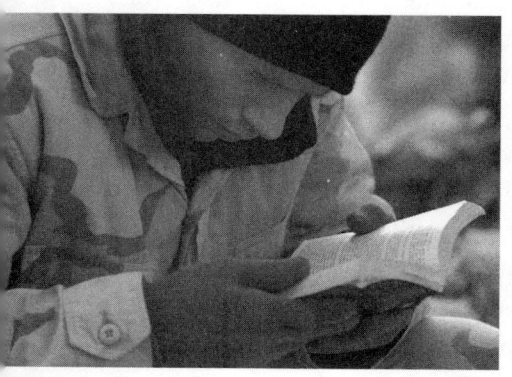

advantages over other female ethnicities. The services tend to homogenize ethnicities into the service culture but still our cultural and ethnic orientation guides or pulls us depending on our awareness or lack of awareness.

Any of these types of things is avoidable through discovering what are the important parts of my life philosophy. Sometimes one's religious training guides well enough, yet unless the underlying philosophy is identified, then religious affections can grow cool quickly. Religious background does not endorse everything we think or do as right. Many a religious person is deeply affected by philosophic orientation. You have simply to look at Northern Ireland, South Africa, or the Middle East for an explanation. A very religious person may be misguided albeit seem "holy" to themselves. Sound like a Taliban?

Bottom line is that my decisions flow from my background. So "Where are you?" in terms of your background? This will identify to you where your options are and lead to you making some personal convictions about life and reality.

DEVELOPMENT OF PERSONAL CONVICTIONS

Personal convictions arrive about the same time as personal crises arrive. And this is the take-off point.

Maybe by the time you've read this far you have begun to rethink who you've become. Perhaps this is the time to start thinking about where you go from here. Many military people find their time in the service is the first time they've had to really get away from their families and think long and hard about their orientation. This again is a good thing.

Standing in a guard post high above Tiger Island, I asked a young soldier about the changes he had experienced since being in the military. "It has made me rethink who I am and what I'm doing in the world," he said. As he peered out over the Pacific sunset scanning for ocean drug runners he relayed the fact that not only had his time in the service given him a new perspective on things, it had made him realize that a lot of the orientation he had been given growing up had been very helpful for him to sort out his personal convictions for his life.

There are many military personnel like this. And there are others who have gained from their military experience and developed new patterns of behavior, life and faith since entering the military. After some time in the military everyone realizes that the "know-it-alls" who couldn't keep their mouth shut during the initial military entrance processing station are gone. By the time you enter your first unit and have been there for a while, you realize that your personal convictions are just that, "your personal convictions." No one else but you is responsible for them and your convictions are as good as the next person's convictions. And if you do not keep yours or develop them, others' beliefs will be dumped on you by people who are more than generous to make you as miserable as they are with their cheap philosophies and crude religious interpretations.

Are your convictions important? You bet they are. They usually surface in or after a crisis too. Because the military is a crisis-response sort of organization, those of us in the uniform of our country end up in or near a crisis frequently. The common military values we hold are for our organizational effectiveness. The convictions you hold are for your personal effectiveness.

Even though our initial entry into the military is a sort of liberation from parents or high school or a dead-end job, the freedom from your personal convictions about your cultural, personal and spiritual orientation is only a temporary freedom. These are your defining characteristics and form the basis for the way you will interact with both your peers and God.

So if you haven't made gone through a thorough questioning process about who you are, and where you've come from, you'll not be able to orient yourself in the terrain of a fast-paced military environment where the weak are eaten up daily by those just looking for easy prey. And if you ignore the questions or the orientation you bring to yourself in the service, then you're not taking advantage of what this time could do for you. It's all about self-improvement and actualization. This is your time to explore, investigate, change and flourish.

I met a classic example of this type of person when I ran into a specialist (Enlisted, 4th class or E4) one day who was in his late twenties. He was evidently very intelligent and showed some interest in something I was saying. When I asked him where he went to school he avoided my questions and didn't want to say anything. After getting more comfortable with our conversation he unveiled that he held a master's degree in both medieval literature and history and had been a fellow in a university history department. Why was he in the military, I asked? "It is a place for me to think things through without the pressure I'm facing on the outside." He was in the process of orienting himself. Something wasn't working for him in the university and so he decided to take a detour into the military to give him some additional time and space to think things through. For this particular soldier, the time in the service was a time for regrouping. He typified to me the perfect example of one who was conscious of orienting himself and settling his convictions about his future and his contributions in life.

MAKING COURAGEOUS CHOICES

It doesn't take a courageous person to go along with the masses. And one of the great lessons in life is that if you do not take advantage of your life and where you are going with it, you will soon arrive and wonder why you wasted so many years getting nowhere. As I said before, crisis has a way of bringing focus to our lives and the military is good at getting involved in crises.

As paratroopers line up on the tarmac to board C-17s at Pope Air Force Base in North Carolina, or as sailors hang over the gunwales of an aircraft carrier waving to loved ones in Virginia Beach or marines board ships in San Diego headed for the Persian Gulf, the issues remain: Where is God in all this? What do I do with my emotions? What should I believe? These ultimate questions may never resolve completely for anyone. Yet each individual ought to have a general idea of how he or she relates to each of these.

You notice that this chapter hasn't told you what to believe as much as it has cautioned you that your disposition may be your greatest asset or hindrance toward answering any of the big questions in life about God. I find the greatest problem with any of these answers is that soldiers and sailors, airmen and marines just hardly get past themselves. If we could step aside and view ourselves from a distance we'd probably see that our cultures and philosophies stand in the way of our believing. They often create the prejudice against God, the church, the Bible and anything religious. Servicemen or women often listen to crude explanations of ultimate truth when they won't listen to a chaplain, a civilian minister or a booklet like this.

I will not tell you what to believe because most service members have more problem with their biases than their beliefs. The soldier in the guard tower in Tiger Island, Honduras, was a youth leader in his church. Once turned soldier, he departed from all those enhancing events and relationships and allowed the Army to drag him into a lifeless spiritual form. He yearned to get back to his faith after he left the military. My question for him was why couldn't he regain that form while in the military? Why is it that so many military people give in to a system which has no power other than what we give it and people allow themselves to become spiritually lifeless and formless? It is a lack of personal courage. One of the Army's key values, but sadly undervalued.

Lieutenant Wall was a handsome Engineer Officer, third generation West Point Officer, and the son of both a General Officer father and a General Officer grandfather. He loved his work as a combat engineer platoon leader but shared a vision for becoming a missionary. While other officers of his grade were blindly following the masses and acting stupidly every weekend, Lt. Wall was making his mark as a Christian in the Army. He participated in chapel events and shared his enthusiasm for faith freely. It took courage for him to embrace his beliefs but he did so continuously and courageously. When his obligation to serve ended, he transitioned to civilian life and continued his goal of becoming a missionary. It wasn't because he was a preacher's kid that this officer pursued his vision, it was because he was courageous enough to make his choice and follow his decision. It would have been very easy for him to continue in the service with such support from his family. Yet he decided to go against what was obvious in his life to something he truly believed in with all his heart.

This is the sort of courage needed in people today. Where young people short themselves is not in a lack of information so much as it is in a lack of courage to ask the tough questions about themselves, which keep them from authentic faith. You don't lack any energy for the same kind of decision this lieutenant made, you simply lack making the decision to do the intellectual work to make the personal assessment and the courage of heart to make a decision.

When Jesus interrupted a group of orthodox religious zealots who were stoning a woman who had been caught in the act of cheating on her husband, his recommendation did not involve several agencies, support groups and workshops. His words were simply, "go and sin no more." The simplicity and power of human decision-making is at the heart of everything about God. After all, I can't convince you of the love of God nor of the great mysteries of the Christian faith. But that isn't as important as the power you hold in your decision-making. Once you "get

off the dime" with your personal initiative, you will begin to discover all sorts of things about yourself, God and the world.

One promise in the Bible given to every person who wants to "seek" God is that they will find him if they seek for him with all their heart.

considerations

Consideration 1: How do you identify yourself and your culture? Do you accept society's labels like "GEN X" or "Grunge" or "Player" or "Straight Edge" or "Vegan" or do you seek to find yourself apart from these? Sometimes labels simply get in the way and keep you looking at the wrong target. Try to define yourself by writing down the stuff you hold on to as yourself. Ask yourself what you would pay for each of those items. Save only the stuff that is the most expensive and toss the rest. Ask yourself the next question of how you actually "portray" the image you say you are.

Consideration 2: Measure your thinking. Do you care enough about your Orientation to read a footnote source? Good, then you're listening. You may be close to discovering something about how you function spirituality! This isn't rocket science, but it might be just as difficult! Measure by determining your energy level about the ultimate stuff. If you are interested you pursue things. If you are seeking, you will spend more time reading than talking. If you are thinking you will do more writing and less jabbering with friends. Good ideas and lasting impressions require capture by thinking, writing or our energy to understand them.

Consideration 3: What are the non-negotiable things for your personal character? Mel Gibson's portrayal of William Wallace in *Braveheart* some years ago brought a new sense of commitment to family and friends like none of us had seen in a long time. What is your non-negotiable stuff? What makes something non-negotiable? Is it a moral quality? Sometimes people get indignant about their lives and simply are stubborn. Whatever is non-negotiable to you ought to also be trans race, gender and creed. Separate you from everything else, determine your convictions, and then seek to find the faith which supports those good qualities you have determined essential. You'll be surprised at the result!

Find and Make Good Friends—People, their power, their influence and their strength.

"a friend sticks closer than a brother"

King Solomon, from the book of the Proverbs

POWER OF FRIENDSHIPS

What do people have to do with God? They're the closest you'll get to God this side of Heaven. But the French philosopher, Jean Paul Sartre, coined the sardonic expression, "les autres, c'est l'enfer" or "others, that's hell." I think I believe both are true. This chapter seems inappropriate in a book about God and faith and yet the more I take stock of why people in uniform do not have faith, it is because of people. And that is a sad reality.

This chapter may be more confessional than directive. But I think I need to tell you about some people that have made a lasting impact on my life. This is like a turning point in *Under Orders*, because I think in order for you to keep reading, you must know more about who shaped my life and thinking and why. You also need to know the mistakes. Maybe in this cross-examination of relationships you can find something similar to your own journey.

It used to be that the technological age was a futuristic imagination of a few good writers. Before FM antennas and television transmission and the possibility of calling overseas on a hard phone line connection, people would sit around and talk about things in the evening after work. In tribal communities in the Far East, Africa, South America and Southeast Asia the tradition of passing stories to younger generations was the way culture, faith, traditions and myths about life were passed along. I used to relish the conversations my grandfather would have with my dad and uncle while I lay sleepily in my mom or dad's lap, listening and laughing to stories from long ago. I didn't understand much of what I heard, but I knew something powerful was going on when that old man would talk. I regret I did not know him for very long before he passed away and I never heard stories like that again. One cassette tape is all that is left from over a half century ago.

The power of learning from mistakes told through tales and gaining life lessons from storytelling is an art passed down from millennia before us. Yet in this techno age, it seems that we don't allot the same leisure of time to learning lessons from people, though we still relish a good story and we learn deeply from the intensity of human emotions and energy put into a tale of betrayal, of intrigue, of opportunities seized and some lost. The current assessment of this generation is that it doesn't care about anything but Xboxes and Playstations, but I don't find that true in my office. It seems that an older generation too quickly devalues the contributions and interests of this current wave of postmodern people. Because some things are better told than taught, I invite you to discover the interesting power of people and faith as they have impacted my life. This could be called "some of the most interesting people I've met" but then you wouldn't read it. Instead, it is all about how God comes to us in people when we least expect it.

In the Old Testament, angels would often assume human form and enter the lives of people you might have heard of, like Abraham, Moses, Jacob and others. A Jewish friend of mine helped me understand this better when he told me that God interrupts our lives sometimes through incidents and people and it is our responsibility to pay attention in order to learn the lesson for our life. Remember Meg Ryan falling in love with an angel played by Nicholas Cage in the movie *City of Angels*? Our imaginations get carried away with the thought that there is another dimension to life and that somehow God might actually interrupt our lives to break in and tell us something. And yet, God does this every day through events and people. I can't prove it but I have lived it. And maybe it's one of those "sixth sense" kind of things where you have to have your eyes opened up before you can see.

During this chapter, give yourself a break and try to think about your life in terms of divine interruptions through people. You might be surprised at who you see appear.

THE DRIFTER

I had no idea where this guy came from or why he was in town but he showed up in my white clapboard New England church one Sunday and tried to look inconspicuous sitting in the back pew. As I greeted people who left the service that morning I greeted him. I didn't ask him any questions. I just looked into his eyes and told him I was glad he was there. I was a young man of about twenty-three at the time and the Drifter was about thirty-five. His young face had deepened wrinkles and he looked scared. I was as surprised as anyone else when he returned a couple of weeks later.

We weren't a military congregation, so we weren't accustomed to people just "falling into" our congregation. In a small church everyone knows everyone else and visitors don't have the luxury of anonymity. The Drifter came back and I took the opportunity to visit him in his small apartment in town and invited him to dinner at the parsonage. He accepted the invitation and came alone to dinner. He was just as quiet at dinner as he was in church and I didn't interrogate him. We had a quiet dinner until he asked me what I wanted. I told him I didn't want anything. I was a pastor and I was just making myself available to him and his family (they hadn't arrived in town yet). He acted surprised at my response and a bit embarrassed. Then he told a tale.

"When I had attended college in Connecticut years ago, I was asking a lot of questions internally about God, his existence, my life, and my spiritual being. I was going to a Christian college so after I didn't get any good conversations with a couple of teachers I decided to go to the school president. I will never forget that day. I entered his plush office and figured that this guy should have what I need to know, after all, he's the president of the college. Haltingly, I opened my mouth and asked how it is that I could know about how to know God and know that my sins were forgiven. I was astonished when after breaking this down in some painful personal detail, I waited for a response and the guy chuckled and told me he really didn't know but maybe I ought to find a pastor somewhere and talk to him." The Drifter's face was sunken and sad. I had the feeling this incident, which had probably taken place some fifteen years previous, might have occurred yesterday. It was so real to him.

After graduation he had married and began a family and moved to the Pacific Northwest. While out there he and his wife had gotten interested in a commune (not the same person as the sergeant's story though). Still being internally spiritually troubled or seeking, the Drifter said that the people at the commune, called "The Way," had been absolutely the greatest of friends at first, taking them places, inviting them to dinner, and surrounding the young family with tons of love. After a while, the Drifter and his wife decided they would join the commune, sell their house, give the proceeds to the organization and begin living in every aspect for the commune. This went on for several years in relative happiness until the Drifter discovered that the leader of the commune was sleeping with most of the women except his wife and that he had another lifestyle as a result of the money of each of the participants.

When he questioned the church leaders, they told him it was okay. Sometimes leaders have to have different rules than the followers. Reaching back into his common sense the Drifter felt this was one of those non-negotiable things and wasn't right regardless of who or where or when. When he continued to surface his objections he was pulled aside and told to be quiet. His objections were not the will of God. Troubled and once again feeling like the man in the big office was laughing at him, the Drifter concocted a plan to leave the commune. When someone in the leadership heard of his plan he was told that his life would be at risk if he left. His heart was breaking because even his little children were devout followers of the church.

When the Drifter slipped into the back pew of my little white church in 1979, he was scared to death. It was the first time in ten years he had been outside the commune. He had returned to something he knew and something he believed in. Yet he was scared because his family was in hiding and he was afraid that any moment someone from The Way would find him, kill him, and end his tortured life. That was what he told me.

I remember that Sunday afternoon like yesterday—him telling this fugitive tale of escape and evasion. But I never saw the Drifter again.

Yet he remains in my mind one of the most remarkable people I've met because of his intensity of faith and because he at least held on with tenacity to his faith. His tale taught me that people don't forget things that have to do with their faith and that their faith is their treasure. It was so critical to him that I be real with him. I told him I would not visit him again because I didn't want to pressure him to attend our church. I let him know he was always welcome there even though to this day I do not know where he went and I never met his wife and children. Last I knew, he was headed in the right direction, not giving up on his spirituality nor allowing others to take it away from him.

People carry their needs with them wherever they go. It doesn't matter if you're flying in a C-130 or if you're hunkered

over a radio set in a re-trans station a thousand miles from the front lines, your life and your life needs are with you. Like the Drifter, you can run but you cannot hide from them. Hopefully, you too will have the savvy to seek the truth and be able to know when something is fake. That too was another lesson from the Drifter, that sometimes you may think your religious orientation is right-on but in reality it might be far afield of center. The Drifter knew that finding the right thing might cost him his life but he valued his life and that of his family.

Since that time, we've all seen a number of sects and cults like Jim Jones and David Koresh's group, come and go. It is always the same result, much sadness and pain. If your religion does not dignify you it is wrong. If your religion does not respect your humanness as limited then it is wrong. If your religion asks you to do something contrary to nature, it is wrong. We have learned since 9-11 that religion per se is not always right.

I learned the importance of letting someone find their way. I learned that even when I wanted to erase years of hurt that continued to haunt this guy, those things would always be part of his spiritual need. Sometimes I wonder whether or not the Drifter was an angel teaching me things I needed to learn about hurting people. Perhaps you have run into people like my Drifter. Perhaps there are some individuals you come into contact with who profoundly challenge your biases and rupture your cultural close-mindedness. Maybe there is some spirituality in your peering into your life for where you've excluded others because of your own preoccupying needs. Perhaps now is a good time to look and listen for something new.

THE PASTOR

A good many people rely on people, like the Drifter did, to guide them to truth. When people can't do it, God gets blamed for the error. Yet the one who suffers the most from this quick lottery of decisions isn't God but the people who need God the most.

Jean Daniel Wohlfahrt, his real name, was a Lutheran pastor in Eastern France when I was a student at the University there years ago. I had moved to France to study systematic theology and had brought along my three children and spouse for what I rightly anticipated would be a delightful several years in Europe living like Chevy Chase and savoring the good life. As anyone knows, Europe can also be hard. There were many cultural difficulties in the 80s having to do with terrorism and the dropping dollar-to-franc exchange rates. And the first winter we were there seemed to be the worst on record for a hundred years and so forth. It was very cold, our apartment bled with condensation on the walls, and yet we attempted to do all the right things to make life happen for our family so that it would be a positive experience.

Part of that was being part of a church. Since my arrival in France, I had been subject to what appeared a comedy of errors in terms of the church I was a member of. And when I got to Strasbourg, the church seemed very interested in itself and not too much interested in me nor my family. I guess this is a common problem with people who travel, like service people, and so I just gritted my teeth with this cool reception and continued to push through knowing that my tour would end sooner or later and I'd get past all of this hard stuff.

Hard went to harder, and colder, and more isolated feeling. Finally I followed my heart and decided to go to another church and take another look at things. I broke out of my focus on one church and began attending another. The people weren't excessively friendly, but by now I was used to it. The church was Lutheran and the pastor was an active, gregarious individual who sought out my apartment and found me and my family in the cold city that winter. While he was talking to me, my daughter—now in the Coast Guard—walked up without warning, pointed to the pink socks and declared they were "great." She returned a few minutes later with identical pink socks to which everyone laughed. Jean Daniel sat her on his lap as we talked. He warmed our hearts with his compassion and concern.

That day I decided to leave my evangelical church to become a Lutheran minister. I realized that day with my daughter that Jean Daniel had done what no one else had cared to do, and that was, care for my family. He found us and connected us to the church in that city. For the rest of my time in Europe Jean

Daniel, was my pastor, guiding me through hard times and celebrating the good times.

The great impressions do not have to be all that theologically deep, they just need to be timely. We are human beings and we need to make connections with other human beings. Even though I was already a minister, I too was a human being and needed to be cared for. Sometimes I think my soldiers forget I'm human! But it isn't a secret I try to hide. We all should be aware of our need for the right kind of things in the church we go to. And rather than execute God for "failure to repair," we ought to allow people to be themselves and find God where we can, as we can.

Jean Daniel taught me that pastors care about people, even about socks. Pastors do not have to be the brightest or the best to carry out God's mission but they do have to be interested in people. And that visit that day told me that that was the kind of church I wanted to be a pastor in one day. It took me fourteen years to become a Lutheran minister after that pastoral call, but I will never forget Jean Daniel.

I will never forget him because he was energetic and because he wasn't appreciated by some of the more intellectual people in the church who insisted on having a pastor with a doctorate instead of just a university degree. In addition, Jean Daniel's picture-perfect wife Marie-Claire was dying from colon cancer. In the midst of having three teenagers, a beautiful but dying wife, and a congregation who detested Jean Daniel's lively and country talk, he still had time to care about my family.

Religious people don't always treat you right, but that doesn't mean all religion is all wrong. And you need to remember is that where you serve in the military your participation in services can help make an impression on people you don't even know. There is a lot of benefit in doing the simple things well. Jean Daniel pastors in France today and his pink socks live on in my heart. He taught me that once in a while we will experience "unexpected goodness" when all around us the world seems to be falling down. Making connections with people brings that goodness home to us.

A MOTORCYCLE

Life started to end for me on a motorcycle. I was extremely depressed over my life and marriage and was uncertain about how to find my way through such a terrible situation. A friend of mine had found the motorcycle on a lemon lot and recommended I purchase it. His method was his madness as the project itself captivated my interest and also provided him time to cycle with me. He knew I was traveling through a difficult period in my career and life and the interest in chrome and horsepower was just the right recipe for a common bond.

When the project was finished I was riding along in the bright sun in Hawaii feeling that despite all the strides I had made, my life was pointless and inconsequential. I felt myself a tremendous failure in not being able to sustain a marriage as I had promised and wanted. I felt I had to get out. It was there in the rush of wind and blur of chrome that I imagined cascading and tumbling into my death and leaving all the details and dilemma to others. My unprotected head was certain to be crushed I figured.

Somewhere in the bright sun and the rush of the open wind a gentle voice reminded me of my children and how much they counted on me. In the same second my hand backed off the throttle and like I was in a dream I slowed remarkably and rode for several miles wondering how close I had come to the stupidity of terminating a perfectly good life which had some painful wrinkles in it.

Part of the healing process was a good friend with the shared passion of motorcycles. Our relationship at work was eclipsed by our periodic cruises around the island. We would always ride places together and would share our interests in the bikes and also share our lives. It seems that this relationship seemed to be a resource for me during my crisis so that it didn't matter whether we ever talked about the subject of my divorce; we spent time together talking about whatever came to mind. Sometimes in our efforts to be spiritual we miss the spirituality of friendship.

Our friendship became our shared resource through multiple crises. Around the focus of our hobby we built our connectedness and sustained ourselves through a three-year tour in a very beautiful island location but demanding job period. Now that we are about to be stationed together again I look forward to rekindling our friendship, which has been only periodic through e-mails over the past many years. Yet in today's technological world we have this capability of sustaining friendships better than ever before. Technology provides us the platform to keep connected.

In Christian theology, there is a concept of confession that says if we confess our sins to God he will forgive us and if we confess our sins to one another we will be healed. It is not just our confession to God that matters. Some people pray to God and then go do whatever they want. But Jewish law stated that our vertical relationship with God was validated by our horizontal relationship with people. Christianity offers us the opportunity to share our lives, not just to pray together, but to share our lives. Often sharing our "burdens," i.e., the emotional baggage which comes with crisis, is a way of deepening our trust together. Had I not had the friendship over that motorcycle, I would have been terribly alone in my pain. The great power and influence of a caring friend is a thing of power in your life. The solidarity provided by that type of relationship is uplifting and renewing to a person's emotional health.

Today, I still ride a motorcycle and often reflect on the goodness of God that came through my friendship. I open this up to you because I think it brings a new perspective to the power of friendships that I don't want you to miss. Friendships in my estimation are sacred things. And sometimes I believe God is present in the exchange of personal information in such a way that it has the effect of healing our deepest needs.

One of the most sought after things by your generation is to be connected to someone in a friendship where there is deep trust. So, this sort of relationship isn't just any old friendship but one where the commitment is deepened by a common sense of the value of a person's contribution to me, and me them. There are also horror stories of soldiers who share something personal too soon and it gets all over the barracks or tales of individuals who take advantage of this "personal-ness" to gain sexual advantage. This isn't what I'm talking about. Those people are thieves and emotional terrorists.

Friendship is gained through long-term trust and sticking together based on common noble values like integrity, solidarity and affection. Even thieves trust each other, but friends trust based upon goodness instead of advantage. Where I thought life would end on a motorcycle, God was there, and where God was, there was also a friend.

PARADE OF PEOPLE

As I mature, I find friends don't always stick together. Time and events have a way of separating us. But there are these intersections of people in my life that I find curiously divine. In the military we live a structured life where most of the people with whom we hang around with are known commodities. For us in the military, there isn't much variety apart from that which we find in our squad, our team or our crew. That's okay because still, there are good people in all these places. The challenge is to hold out and find them.

There are also the low-life people too. You know them. You might be one of them too? They care mostly about themselves. You can't take their word for anything. You can think you have an agreement with them and they will lie about your claims.

They steal partners, sleep with anyone that smells right, and don't seem to quibble about morals. Morals are whatever you think is right to do at any given time. People like this inhabit all units and even get promoted before you do!

It forms what I call the "parade" of people. My mother, who just turned eighty-five, never used a word of profanity in her life. But she decided she had seen enough corruption and wrong-handed dealings of people until one day she did a "Kevin Spacey" and looked up on the wall behind a customer service desk and read a sign which said, "Some people are no damned good." That struck her as prophetic and she began to leak this mantra at the appropriate points when a little advice was needed in the family. Mom is right for the most part. The challenge is to each service member to prove her wrong. The challenge is to do better than the norm; which is something Mom learned after eighty years of trying to work with people.

Despite the rabble of those who don't place value on their relationships with people, there will always be an endless parade of people in your life. Some will seem innocuous to you and others will impress the socks off you. Nonetheless, remember the rule of evidence from Jewish theology—your horizontal life and relationships impact on your vertical relationship with God. Christianity, based firmly in Jewish concepts and theology, is not to be lived in a vacuum. One cannot be a secret Christian in other words.

My theology should impact on those around me. All positive world religions must include a high estimation of the individual. I think Christianity leads the way in this respect[14] due to its

---

[14] I also think that other religions like B'hai and Shintoism respect individuals whereas religions like Islam have degraded views of women and individuals who do not believe the way the Koran teaches. However, all peoples do not necessarily support the entirety of their sacred documents. Just as many Christians do not follow the teachings of Jesus, so there are many Hindus who have a deep respect for individuals as well. This is more a study in comparative religions which is a bit far afield from the purpose of what I'm about here. More can be read on this by looking into Comparative Religions as an index search on the Internet.

insistence on the cause and effect relationship Jesus always insisted on. "If you give a cup of cold water in my name, you do this unto me" for instance. Some other aspects are more self-oriented, like "do unto others as you would have them do unto you." Nonetheless appealing to a selfish perspective, it encourages even self-centered people to be nice to others. If my theology doesn't integrate how I interact with people then I should drop it and begin searching for one that does.

Whatever the result of your spiritual and theological search, remember the role people play in your life. I think the biggest issue with people is that for most service members, people "get in the way" and produce the greatest hindrance to finding God when it ought to be the other way around. This speaks to those in leadership too. I have met some superb enlisted leaders who supported their military units faithfully and others who played it down. However, when the bullets start to fly as they did in Afghanistan after 9-11, the leaders supported the chaplains providing services on the tarmac at Bagram Air Base. Most leaders are developed along the way. As you read this, consider your role in the military and the impact you have on younger soldiers. Rather than being a son-of-a-bitch, you could be known as a courageous spiritual leader by ensuring your sailors and airmen are battle ready in the event they must face their death.

I will never forget Command Sergeant Major Jesse Laye sitting in chapel every Sunday when I served with the 10th Mountain Division at Ft. Drum long before we deployed to Operation Restore Hope. Jesse always set the example to soldiers by going to chapel. He wasn't excessively religious, but he always supported my services in the field and then modeled a leader's contribution to religious support. Jesse was one of those sergeants major who was every bit the model soldier, he had every Army school imaginable and had deployed to combat with the Rangers. His dream job was the Regimental Sergeant Major of the Rangers, which he did in 1995, and went on to serve several four-star generals before retiring. Chief of Staff of the Army, General Eric Shinseki said of Laye, "If I could trade reputations with anyone in the Army it would be Jesse Laye." I hope young enlisted soldiers and sailors, marines and airmen will strive to be as professional and as courageous as Jesse Laye and bring the personal spiritual courage to their lives that he brought.

Jesse was one of those bright stars in my life. He passed through and left some good things in me, which I retain to this day; things like courage of convictions, never-quit stamina, brute honesty, and most of all, care for the soldier. Without being super religious he lived a life of faith and tried to model it the best he could.

Sometimes you will find faith hard to express and tougher to live. But if you watch these great examples that parade by, you can pick up some terrific tools for managing your fledgling spirituality. I knew that Jesse Laye cared about soldiers deeply because everything he did he did to ensure their survivability on the battlefield. When it came down to him explaining how he felt about the soldiers one day, he said, "I think the world of those young guys and girls out there." I knew from the seriousness of his tone he thought of them more as his children than as employees of the United States government.

I was traveling through Chicago's O'Hare airport some time ago and had one of those curiously divine intersections I spoke of earlier. My wife was standing waiting for me and five feet away from her a friend I hadn't seen in twenty-seven years, my first college roommate, now pastor of the Donnellson Fellowship Church in Nashville, Tennessee, Rob Morgan. Neither of them knew the other and as I walked toward my wife I suddenly reached out and grabbed the arm of this man standing in a black trench coat. He whirled around and gasped as his eyes met mine and we immediately embraced. He had told me by telephone years before that if I needed him to call him and he would be on a plane immediately. I had passed through many crises without Rob, and that day we renewed the passion of a spiritual friendship that began in a college dormitory.

Whatever your direction in life, you cannot afford to miss the people who make up this life. I truly believe the reason we are challenged to live the Gospel is that God wishes to live his sacredness through us, for we are the closest thing to God anyone has ever seen.

considerations

Consideration 1: Where has God tried to interrupt your life? This is the toughest question of all, but the most rewarding too. Recognition of the divine in your life is a way of saying that God is involved in your life. If you believe you've met some truly remarkable people but you aren't convinced God was in them or sent them, then who did? And where does that "good" quality come from? People are both good and bad, yet some people defy logic and are simply holy, sacred.

Consideration 2: Sharing your life isn't easy. How can you know a person is safe to share your life burdens with? This has to be a composite answer. And it can vary so much too. Sometimes, people just "connect" as if they've known each other for their entire lives. Other times people seem to grow in confidence with each other. As you determine this, ask yourself what are the non-negotiable things that must be established before a safe friendship can be made?

Consideration 3: Do you have a faith? And do you live your faith towards others? The ultimate test of any religion is its durability with people. Perform a "system check" on your belief system. What does it say about others? Jean

Paul Sartre, the philosopher, was not a theologian so his "others are hell" remark may be true in one sense. But what sort of religion you possess is easily identified by how you value and treat others. This is religious practice at its best. Where do you put your value, on people or on your own agenda? How do you treat others?

Understand the End—Death comes to everyone, sometimes unexpectedly and sometimes anticipated, nonetheless, it will come.

"the difficulty my friends, is not to avoid death, but to avoid unrighteousness"

Socrates, the Apology

DEATH IS SO FINAL.

The crazy thing about military life is that it constantly deals with death. We are either inflicting death upon someone or we are memorializing those who have died. Although we sterilize our profession with the terms *military* and *service*, our profession is called the "profession of arms" and entails all those aspects of breaking things and killing people on the battlefield to achieve an end that diplomacy fails to reach. It isn't a profession of killing, but a profession of arms. The difference is that in the military when we use violence we have at least a higher objective in mind than a murderer in the dark shadows of a homicide somewhere. Our military profession seeks to keep the peace through strength. That often involves destruction, killing and the deaths of brave uniformed individuals.

Death is one of the top three issues service members are concerned about when asked their issues. The other two are their future and relationships.[15] Everyone wants to know more about death; what happens when we die? What is the nature of death? Where do we go when we die? Many questions we cannot answer. What we can answer is that when it comes to us in the military, we are treated with the utmost dignity and respect. And this is not by chance.

In fact, one of the reasons the US Military is so insistent on treating their dead comrades in arms so reverently is that firstly our culture values human lives and secondly that military men and women can know they will not be left behind to rot or be disfigured by the enemy on the battlefield. They can know that their body will be guarded and draped in their country's flag and returned to home and family and given a burial befitting their noble service. It encourages bravery when people know they will be revered if they fall under hostile fire.

One of the biggest problems with death is it is unacceptable. It doesn't fit with how we view life. But it occurs every day. Most people don't get near dying people or death and so to be exposed to a situation with blood and loss of life is a terrifying experience. Yet to those who make their living on a farm or in a trauma unit, death just occurs as the result of accident, failure to survive, or as a matter of fact. And death is a matter of fact. It will come, sooner or later to each of us.

I seem to find myself near people who are near death more often than I would like—I don't care for death much myself

---

[15] In informal sampling of groups I engage with indicates that the top three are in order: 1) relationships, 2) my future, and 3) death and mortality. Even though the age group of 18-25 is totally consumed by being young and carefree, much of the concern has to do with their mortality. A generation whose trademark seems to be multiple tattoos and piercing betrays their concern about the meaninglessness of a life without an identity, and a life without pain. Yet for the most part, their inflictions of pain are controlled and mild. Suicidal teens continue to be another group and not representative of the entire generation.

either! As a chaplain, I am often there when conveying a message from the Red Cross about a death, or explaining to a family member the circumstances around a death. And people's reactions, though similar to a degree, always seem to affect me. Regardless of the number of times I have looked into the eyes of the survivors, those who grieve over death always mirror back to me a glimpse of my own future grief over a parent, a child, a loved one who might die. It is a haunting thing, somewhat mythic, somehow bigger than just a physical "giving out." Death has both physical, spiritual and mythic proportions.

There is always something heart-wrenching when watching someone at a military funeral receive the flag, ceremonially wrapped and tucked with special care, white gloves running over every corner to insure it is perfectly blue and white. The red and white stripes must not be visible. Only the blue color of honor is visible. Sacrifice and courage are within. As the officer in charge of the detail bends down to present the folded colors, the flag is designed to tumble softly into the arms of the deceased's family member. That tumble seems so much bigger than it is. As the words "…of a grateful nation" are uttered, the triangle lifts and plops downward into the waiting arms of a wife or husband, their tear drenched eyes blinking to offer a whispered "thank you" to the uniformed individual. No matter how many times I have observed this holy moment, I am always riveted by the strong symbolism of how powerful a life is when it is honored by its country in such a ceremonial way.

Most people never see that moment but once or twice in life and usually later in life. But it happens every day.

If death is unacceptable, we do a good job in the military of making it reasonable, or honorable, or memorable. If not, death would be a horrifying and meaningless end. Once again, the military illustrates things that are not visible in the civilian world. When I pastored churches before entering the military, if an individual died and did not have a particular faith, I would perform a generic service and do my best to dignify the individual's passing, trying to make sense of it in spiritual terms to a grieving family. But when a service member is laid to rest there is this overwhelming sense of fulfillment that permeates everyone in the military "detail" (the detachment of soldiers or sailors who perform the honors duty) and strikes the family by surprise.

Hollywood has in my opinion done a pretty good job of conveying an understanding of death and what it might be like. In many films there is the tendency toward an intermediate state where individuals who die also return to attempt to make contact with their lovers or families. In some cases the dead are seen as ordinary people walking around attempting to finish things. In others, they are mythic voices or urges that cause the living to realize that we live forever and that there is no need for fear of death. I like the films because I think there are elements of truth in each of them though I subscribe to a more "biblical" understanding of death. I don't know for sure what will occur after death but I think I do. And the one concept I think is very consistent in Christian theology is that we all live forever.

IMMORTAL MAN AND THE PROBLEM OF LIVING

Well, there might be problems with living forever too. At least if it means we must live here in this world forever. One of the best books apart from the Bible I have ever encountered and read more than one time, is the book *All Men Are Mortal* by Simone de Beauvoir, French historian and philosopher.[16]

---

[16] Simone's book in French is entitled, *Tous les hommes sont mortels*, published by Editions Gallimard (1946). Simone writes from an existentialist philosophic viewpoint which at the conclusion of World War II was the prevailing philosophy of the day. Existentialism reduces meaning to that of the individuals' importance and encourages individuals to live for the moment because only the moment has meaning. There are still existentialist hangovers today. Philosophies do not die, they just get replaced by newer versions and varieties. That is why I mention postmodernism, which follows after existentialism.

Simone wrote her novel about a fictional character named Fosca, who discovered an elixir that would give him immortality. He drinks the elixir and discovers he had miscalculated the effects of being immortal as he buries family after family and conquers army after army only to have to conquer new armies. Fosca at first thirsts for conquering armies and countries but ultimately grows weary of this as he realizes that every age brings a new challenger who is bolder and braver than the last. He becomes cynical of bravery, of the thirst for fame, and of the thirst for power. It ultimately is for nothing to the immortal Fosca. Yet death becomes his desire. Life becomes torture as he sees the same sorts of characteristics in men and women age after age. Greed, avarice, hate, love, revenge are repeated by countless civilizations without anyone learning or changing after hundreds of years of living. He finally reaches exasperation and wishes to die but he cannot. The evil side of the elixir requires him to live in order to see that death would have spared him his immortal torture. He concludes that the only good of man is to be faithful to his own conscience.

More than any other book, *All Men Are Mortal* helps me to understand graphically the benefits of death and my own miserable mortality. There are reasons built into life which make sense of death. Though not apparent to us at first, after a while, death begins to make a sort of sense to end suffering and pain, to end what is futile and to bring to final rest an individual or family suffering from a horror or fear. And so, perhaps death isn't as bad as it first seemed when this chapter began. Maybe there are some benefits to this thing of death.

But dying presents its own problems because we still are left with so many questions about the nature of death. Yet though death is natural, it doesn't necessarily have a nature because it isn't a person, it is a condition. Death occurs to individuals. And so the focus needs to shift to us as individuals rather than death as an abstract concept alone. The conditions of being alive or dead both have characteristics to them. Here is where I turn to get more theological in this book. And that is because I don't have any other document that is clearer on this subject for me than the scriptures of the Old and New Testaments and the theology which is based on them. I will talk more about my reliance on that as a meaningful source later in Order Eight.[17] That involves the subject of epistemology, or "how we know." For now, it is sufficient to grasp that if a source for meaning is used consistently and that source is consistent within itself, then it is probably pretty good. However there is one more thing about the Bible that makes it more meaningful than just another book, and that is the involvement of Jesus Christ with the book. All the questions and issues surrounding the life and death of Jesus are significant here.

If the resurrection of Jesus did not occur then much of what follows is simply just argument to a point. However, if that resurrection did occur and the documents which attest it speak the truth, then we probably ought to give it some serious consideration. One of the great qualities about postmodern men and women is that they are willing to hear an argument, but even more, they are willing to hear an underdog. At this point, owing to my style, Jesus is the underdog. Keep reading.

Rather than approach this subject in a purely intellectual fashion or like a systematic theological treatise, I would rather approach it from some simple perspectives and build my thoughts around the framework of how we understand life and death. It seems as I often interact with soldiers, that the same

---

[17] If you're wondering why I rely on the Bible, it is because of my epistemology. Chapter 8 will take up this in a more significant way. However, if you can't wait, realize that all truth claims are established by their believability. All the claims of Christian theology from the Bible ultimately are based on two things: 1) the reliance on a book of documents called holy scripture which comes with obvious attestations as to its reliability both from the Masoretic tradition of the Jewish culture, and 2) the reliance of Jesus Christ, the Jewish Rabbi and self-proclaimed redeemer of mankind whose resurrection alone validates his claims. If you struggle with the resurrection, you're not alone, however you must look at the truth claims to that too. And that comes in chapter 8. Once you see some of the claims you will gain more of a sense of reliance on the claims of Jesus Christ and of the New Testament.

four anxieties about life surface, and these four anxieties are all part of the "death" category: fear, pain, loneliness and rejection. You could refer to these as the death matrix. For in a sense each of these are part of our human condition, that after our theological "fall from grace" in the garden of Eden[18] we were subject to these aspects of death while living, as a harbinger of the future.

Fear pervades our minds and works on our physical bodies as well. We can be afraid in the dark, but we can also fear our destiny, fear the outcome of a war, or fear the worst though still unaware of what that could be. Fear seems to be an uncontrollable entity all its own. It is the great invisible dragon we seek to slay by slogans like "NO FEAR" on t-shirts. Today's "extreme" sports are an indicator of the desire of people to surmount their fears. There is an adrenaline rush to conquering fear. Standing on the top of a forty-foot tower at an Air Assault course, young soldiers would be terrified to step off backward for fear of falling. They were harnessed and belayed and had two ropes running through their figure-eight carabineers but they shook with fear. In order to demonstrate the reliability of the belay system we would often have an instructor jump off the tower cinched only by his two-rope connection. The instructor would hold his hands straight out from his body and demonstrate the reliance of the system. Students would still shake from fear.

Fear is not just conquerable based on the logic of understanding a system. Fear of flying, fear of bridges, animals, crowds and other non-animate situations are real. Yet the service members fear the horror of fighting in combat, of missiles, of the terror of a biological or chemical attack on the battlefield or aboard a ship. Our fears are the edge of our life, where life ends and mortality takes over. We fear that which we cannot

---

[18] Whether literal or figurative, the story of the Fall, as it is called in theology, is the story of a choice made by Adam and Eve in which they "fell from grace" and were "enlightened" though expelled from the presence of God and out of the Garden to a life under the power of sin and its power, death.

control and we do not understand. And when it comes to eternity, we fear the dark aloneness which comes with it.

Pain is also part of the edge of death and mortality. This has become part of the extreme involvement craze as individuals seek to engage in activities that assault them and cause injury. The mosh-pits or punk fights inflict pain. Pink is assaulted by a stray punch in one of her videos *Just like a Pill*. Pain is a sure way of knowing, of feeling, of being alive. Pain brings us to the edge of death without dying. We are allured by the piercing throb pain brings as long as it is controlled and doesn't go too far. We can enjoy a momentary pain. Some sadomasochists use pain to bring them to the euphoria of sexual delight by inflicting a pain that borders on death and yet causes delight. The delight is because there is a return to life. Pain leading to ultimate death is not fun!

Momentary "party-pain" is a wake-up call for people living in a techno-intense world to feel alive. And that is the curious part of this sort of pain. Yet there is another pain that isn't party oriented and that is the pain of loss, failure and doom. Long after the throb of the party pain is over the other more hideous pain can creep into a person's mind and soul and bring them to the verge of suicide and dark death. These pains are often unaddressed and unheard. Many a sailor can feel the deep pain in their heart as they sleep, a pain they do not have to reveal to their shipmates. As we grow older, these pains become our preoccupation, our obsession, and our deep secret. Pains often grow into patterns, and patterns into lifestyles. All because we are subject to the power of death and have no power over it.

Loneliness is a strong cousin to pain and fear, whose lance seems to penetrate deeply in the military community. As much as we seek to bring our ranks to cohesion and build a family, a team, or a sense of belonging, there are always those deep strains of emotional pain called loneliness that drag heavily on a young person's soul. In fact, loneliness is one of the emotions present both in this phase of life and in the last phase. The fear of being alone at death, without friends and family, is an abject fear of the elderly. In Beauvoir's book, Fosca is terrified by the loneliness he feels as his wife combs her hair and proclaims she is losing her beauty though he is still a young man, ageless, and virile. He protests his wife's antipathy of him and his immortality. She only wishes he would age and die with her, but he cannot. And he falls into an endless life filled with the haunting aloneness which keeps him from ever being able to share his life with another human being. Sharing a life would mean to share the events, the pains, the successes and the like experiences which help us to identify and "know" things in our hearts for certain. But once alone, Fosca cannot "know" and he cannot share his life with anyone without being unwanted in the end.

This feeling of loneliness can sweep over people's minds and hearts in the midst of a busy aircraft carrier. Five thousand personnel live aboard one of these huge behemoth nuclear carriers when the combat flyers and support teams are attached to them. A city afloat, these carriers patrol oceans and provide theater strike capability to operations in the Persian Gulf, the Mediterranean and the Far East. And within this city sailors are assigned and work and yet may possess a heart-aching lonely life, devoid of personal contact. Often sexual advances by sailors who cross the barriers of the rules aboard try to make up for the heartache, but it doesn't go away. This loneliness is part of the ache of death. Sometimes sailors would rather die than face loneliness. It can be ignored but it doesn't go away unless it is purged away by hope.

The final aspect of death follows close behind loneliness, as it does Fosca whose immortality caused him to be rejected by every wife he knew. Rejection is one of the leading causes of suicide and violent crimes, as individuals feel unwanted and undesired. It is the single most powerful ally of death. In terms of today's postmodern and millennial generation, rejection is the arch-enemy of relationships—one of the most desired things in this generation. And people cannot handle being rejected because it is like an assignment to death. No one should be rejected either by virtue of the obvious things, like color, creed, or religion, nor by personal bias, preference, clubs, cliques, or rumors. Yet it occurs repeatedly and especially in our military where close-quartered living and rivalry of rank and status constantly bear down on people and turn them into barracks "rats" not wanting interaction with people or activities, which could help resuscitate them to life.

Rejection is a theme throughout history too. It isn't unique to the millennial age. It is a common human dilemma, again, one of the cousins to death.

Fear, Pain, Loneliness and Rejection erode the living and bring them near death. Even if the death is not physical it is emotional, it is mental, and it is spiritual. Have you thought that perhaps the death Jesus talks about in the Gospels has something to do with death in the present? The fact is, many sermons speak of only the death of our bodies and the punishment of our souls. Many a country preacher has preached that sermon! Yet the death that is more illusive is the death that people live in day after day, a death based on their lives of fear, pain, loneliness and rejection. That death is unending. It often drives people to take their lives. That is a final death.

LIFE IS INTANGIBLE.

The only tangible thing about us is that we are a form of dust. We are essentially 75 percent water and about 25 percent material. Physically, we are built this way and we are mortal creatures. The Clonaid Society attempted several years ago to suggest that we have been sired from extra-terrestrial beings. That makes for great publicity, but it flies in the face of thousands of years of history and archaeology to the contrary.

Christian thinking holds to the position that our lives are made from dust and will return to dust. The Eagles were right, "all we are is dust in the wind." In that we are dust, life is temporal.

Life itself is also described in the Hebrew term for breath, *ruach*. We are breathed into existence. In that we are creatures into whom "breath" is breathed, we are eternal.[19] Eternal creatures living in a temporal world.

Life is the essential quality that makes us different from animals who are not breathed creatures, but have breath. Human beings are truly remarkable creatures who have the capacity to live like all the animal kingdom in their human activities, and yet have this added capacity to not simply think, but to think about themselves, to think about the possibility of a god in the universe and to propose extremely sophisticated concepts about god, philosophy and our existence in the world. And, as we are eternal creatures, we will live on after our temporal existence here is over. How and what that looks like are not as clearly delineated in Christian scriptures. We know that it will be an existence without time yet with all the same sensory functions we have now albeit in an eternal realm where God is. That existence is to be one of happiness, joy,  peace and no tears, no pain. Life is a glimpse of the possibilities of this sensation, yet with all the negative elements included.

So when I describe life, it is something bigger than ourselves, and bigger than where we are right now. It has another phase to it with many new dimensions. And life now isn't something cheap to be carelessly squandered as if all there is to life is

---

[19] Technically, theologians would say only God is eternal because God never began, God always has been and will be (in the expression of our "time" concept). We are technically considered "everlasting" because we began at a point in time and will always then exist whether in this world or in the next.

what I now feel or think. Life takes on the quality of being worth living as opposed to being expended. And if life has this sort of value, then we who have life suddenly have something of greater value than material things whose warranty expires after so many days and years.

Life and Its Phases

One of the most challenging aspects to life is its phases. This is really important to understanding how we make sense of our spirituality in what appears to be a world of pain, fear and death. The phases of life seem frustrating at first, like when an 17-year-old still can't get a driver's license but is allowed to join the military. And then once in the military, isn't allowed to consume alcohol. Phases of life are a fact of our human lives and it is often very hard for young service members to realize how they can fit all this talk about eternal things into a life that is bordered by the limitations of life's phases.

And it isn't like once you're an adult, everything is free and easy. Life continues to present phased challenges long after you're old enough to join the service and die for your country! I think the secret to these phases is managing their impact on me. Every time you turn around in life, people are either categorizing you or assigning you to a phase. This is our difficulty with being creatures in a temporal world. We have no other way of understanding each other than to determine where we are on the long continuum of life and determine what we should be doing and thinking at that time. Our cultures also buy into this and help us to determine choices that are best for us on the basis of that continuum. In other words, it really doesn't make sense if a kindergartner wants to marry, and it makes less sense if a mother with four children wants to be single and bar-hop. Some of these things by virtue of our culture restrict us to certain lanes for our own good. When we don't buy into those

lanes we get into cultural trouble and personal crisis that neither god nor country can help us with.

So these phases of life are manageable periods of time. They
are manageable in the sense that the more you see the big picture around you the better you will be able to integrate yourself
and function in the present. This is one of the single most powerful aspects for young military people, who often get the
trapped feeling of having committed themselves to a certain
enlistment period and feel that their entire life is lost. It isn't
lost, it is just that when pain, fear, loneliness and rejection hit
during a phase like service commitment, it is very difficult for
young people to see the larger picture of life. Often the reaction
to the crises these four harbingers of death bring is a reaction of
hopelessness and dejection over being trapped. And yet the trap
is in the mind, which has not grappled with the complexities of
your being both an eternal and physical human creature in a life
phase you feel trapped in.

Managing efficiently involves not simply seeing the "big picture of things," but understanding your significance in the
midst of these phases. You must believe in your essentially eternal quality, which lives far beyond the present. There is more to
you than meets the human eye!

For many years as a chaplain I was assigned to hard light
infantry training, which involved countless deployments and
exercises in the mud, rain, snow and jungle heat. I realized as I
entered this training that the deployments were going to wear
heavily on me if I didn't manage them correctly. So, using a
psychological tool borrowed from my training, I began to
"reframe" my experience. I decided that all these training
events would be a vehicle for my own personal spiritual enrich-
ment. That's right! By reframing the temporal setting in which
I found myself, I was able to invest myself in a creative sense
every time I went to the "field" to train. I think this same principle is a great way for service members to manage the horrible
pace of operations we are thrust into these days. If you wait for

the service to help you with the pace of operations, you'll be waiting for nothing. Perhaps now you can begin reframing your current military life phase into a manageable piece of time. Instead of wallowing in your enlistment decision and balking against the system and possibly hurting your short-term future with questionable moral decisions, you can use this phase of your life to grow and develop. You must remember that not only are you made of dust, you are eternal too. And you will outlive your enlistment.

Dust leads to death, but eternal leads to eternal life. Your current life today is not the end of you. It is a phase in the continuum of time in your life. What is great about the military experience is that it typifies all of life into a three-, four-, or six-year enlistment period. In that period of time you are able to experience this incredible process of transformation of yourself, training and accomplishment (all the phases of life) in one encapsulated block of measurable time. This period will end for you one day. And yet you will live on through many more phases of life, none of which will probably be as more choreographed as this one was.

It is only when you exit the military that you realize how formative it has been for you. In the same way that we manage this military phase of our lives, we can manage our temporal lives. In managing ourselves, we begin to conquer the power of death over our lives. When we realize that we are spiritual, we begin to dislodge the power of fear and pain. But managing is only part of the power, the Gospel is the other part.

Good News for Phase Managers

I agree that life isn't easy. That is a well-known axiom. And managing my phases isn't easy either. I often talk with my adult children in the military and discover once again how hard these phases of life are. Yet I remind myself that it is good to be a mortal creature at least. The difficulties they face won't last forever,

I keep reminding them. Life has a way of settling its deathly dust over our best laid plans and aspirations. And there come times when you can't break out of the fog and see any light. I've been there.

We're all human creatures, some made with more aspiring temperaments than others. God blesses some people with buoyant, irrepressible personalities that seem to float through life without a care. Others find themselves mired in the mountainous detail of objections. And still others seem captivated by fear and suspicion. Depending on your personality type,[20] you may be more or less successful with managing your life than the next person. Everybody has some difficulty. Investigate more about yourself by looking up this topic on the internet at **www.kiersey.com** for more information. There is a great deal to learn about how we function as human beings on that Web site. And it is all self-explanatory. You will enjoy it.

My emphasis here though is on the spiritual side of the human dimension. There are many tools to facilitate your managing your life better and more efficiently and yet there is another dimension that is completely spiritual which has a great deal of energy and power for you too. And that is the good news.

When I say good news, I'm talking about the Good News of the Gospel as given in the Bible. I like this category because it is really simple. And the power of the Gospel is that it doesn't depend on anything or anybody. It is a stand-alone product for everyone who is interested in discovering it.

---

[20] I strongly encourage every service member to consult with their chaplain about taking a Myers-Briggs Personality indicator assessment. Of all the helpful things in life, the Myers-Briggs is the single most powerful tool to assist you in understanding yourself in the world. Once you realize that it is your "type's" tendency to feel depressed or rejected then you can work to free yourself realizing that it isn't just "you" who is creating the problem but the way you are made which is the complexity to the problem. Service members spend so much energy and time in misunderstanding just this simple thing which can help in clarifying their personal understanding of themselves and their lives with others. Truly, the Myers-Briggs is the most powerful tool apart from a lightning bolt which can change your life within a very short period of time!

The good news bottom line is that "death has lost its sting" over human beings. For me as a Christian that Gospel is the message of the Rabbi Jesus who declared that "whoever believes in me will have eternal life." I believe Jesus' resurrection from death on the cross is good news in the face of death. Jewish culture and theology is resurrection focused. Christian theology, derived from Jewish culture, tradition and scriptures, believes that when Jesus was raised from the dead, he conquered the power of death completely. This historic act is today conveyed to us in a real spiritual way by the power of our believing.

Believing in anything is powerful, but like we learned a bit before, is not always validly true due in large part to the problems of epistemology (Order Eight). Yet, when we believe in the good news of the resurrection, we suddenly are focused on something that transcends death and life itself. Christians and Jews both believe in resurrection, that there will be a life hereafter and that it will be good, full of joy and peace. However, it is needed right now!

My Christian theology teaches me that Jesus Christ brings to me a life power that energizes my hope in the midst of these negatives of fear, pain, loneliness and rejection. The hope of the Gospel is that Christ can bring me through the death-matrix of these four deathly elements into a present experience of hope no matter how big or how devastating the circumstances appear. And that is the Gospel—new life now, based on resurrection hope, which Jesus Christ promises to all those who simply believe his power is for them. That is the entire story of Christian theology all in one sentence.

The Gospel, the good news, suddenly brings with it purpose for any phase of life I find myself in, meaning for any circumstance, and hope despite the difficulties and meaningless destination I seem to find myself in. Everybody needs good news. Especially in the military profession. We are such a programmed institution that sometimes it is as if nobody has a personality sometimes. But that isn't true. There are pockets of bright human personality aboard ships and in air wings where people have discovered the good news and are living with hope. The military isn't church, so don't expect everyone to be enthusiastic about your discovery of the good news! But then, don't be discouraged, good news is good medicine against the death-matrix.

Fundamentally, it is up to you to make the difference in determining how you will interact with the natural power of things. Only you can manage any of this. You and your willingness are key.

One of my dear friends is the wife of the most senior ranking Rabbi Chaplain in the U.S. Army. We were talking some time ago about the terrorist bombings in Tel Aviv and the horrible mutilations occurring every day somewhere in Israel. Bracha is one of those beautiful Israeli women with olive skin, dark black eyes and rich long dark hair and reminds me of a biblical character I might have read about in the Prophets somewhere. She said to me, "Bill, we have to remember that in spite of the terrible day-to-day suffering that as long as we have hope, we can persevere to a new day." As a Jew, she understands that hope is central to life. Without hope we are lost in fear and in pain. With hope we know that some day God will bring justice and redemption to Israel and to the world.

As a Christian, I believe that this hope is central to your life as a temporal creature, just like Bracha said. Hope conquers death and all of its power. Even as death is inevitable and unacceptable, hope is inevitable and acceptable to those who believe it is for them. You must manage to believe in the hope of resurrection in order to conquer the futility and inevitability of death. Like the character Fosca determined in *All Men are Mortal*, your single most significant decision will be to your own conscience in any matter and in this matter, it will be ultimately determine if you have hope in the face of death.

considerations

Consideration 1: Determine your view of yourself in the world. Upon what do you base your concept of human beings? This is so important to everyone. During the Communists' rule of power in Russia and East Germany, human beings existed to serve the god of the state. Western thinking isn't like this. Human beings are intrinsically made in the image of God, or at least that is where we derive our sense of their value. In a lecture years ago at the Institute of Human rights in Strasbourg at the L'institute des droits des hommes, a young Chinese girl suggested that all reality was in the state, to which another attendee from the Ukraine stood up and brilliantly declared, "Our human rights are not based in economics but in the essential worth and dignity of human beings." Though more legal than our discussion here entails, this highlights the impact of just assuming that there is nothing more to human beings than our being made out of dust. Fundamental essence of mankind depends on our being made in the *imago dei*, the image of God.

Consideration 2: Why is it so important for you to feel pain in your life? And, are you addicted to pain? Physical pain is appearing in today's culture as the common denominator and starting place for people's reference points. However, I think that will quickly change as the war on terrorism continues to inflict pain again and again on us. Somehow we need to move from self-inflicted pain as a common denominator to the pain of others as a common denominator. Why are we so focused on ourselves?

Consideration 3: The feeling of lost-ness is sometimes overwhelming. We can many times be lost in a crowd. What is the answer for me when I cannot break free of the power of death over me in this feeling? More and more this generation and those of the generations ahead and behind it, are realizing the impact of psychology, pastoral counseling and medicine in helping cope with feelings which paralyze. If you are one of those people whose struggle isn't clarified and resolved reading through a work like this, then perhaps you should consider seeing someone who can help guide you through the troubled waters. Don't be afraid to ask the questions about yourself. For a good number of the service people I talk to, they haven't had the enjoyment of being able to "flesh things out" with someone who helped them resolve them. Seek and you shall find.

ORDER SEVEN

Fight the Real Fight—Sin is irrelevant in today's world, but it still makes its impression on each of us.

"sin is a mistake I make, like a lapse in judgment, or a bad choice"

an assumption I often hear

MISSING THE TARGET

Sin pops its head up in the strangest places. On a bright sunny Grecian day near Athens, a father and son were probably out practicing one of the arts of soldiering. They set up a target and paced their distance to the ready line. Dad would go over the details of archery and talk in detail about the nature of the bow and the importance of a good grip and steady forearm. His little kid probably just wanted to get on with the whole thing but listened patiently just in case Dad might tell him something he didn't already know about the art of firing this curious weapon. Then there is the demonstration, the crack of the bowstring and the jet whisper of the arrow cutting the space and the crisp impact of an arrow hitting the makeshift target. It is an incurable thing to want to hit a target. For some it is easier than others. This day, it is the kid's chance to shoot.

As his Dad wraps his arms around him to steady him, the little boy is eager with anticipation. Coached by his experienced Dad, they both release the arrow and it finds its destination, penetrating firmly into the target. The next try is solo, the little kid now holds the bow, which is larger than himself, and tries to steady his grip. Dad provides a bit of steadying while the kid readies everything to shoot, the forearm, the fingers—now aching from the bowstring's draw, the eye on the sight, and the target—now curiously moving back and forth in his view, something it hadn't done with Dad's help. "Release!" his Dad orders him and the arrow lobs haphazardly over the target into the grass nearby. A disappointed child looks up at his Dad and asks, "What happened?" His Dad replies, "You sinned." Sin from the word *hamartia* in Greek, is pictured by the failure of a weapon to strike its target, most commonly in Greek times, an arrow missing its target. This word from the Koine Greek, the common Greek spoken in the streets, is the word from which all our conversations about sin come. Without getting extremely technical, this is where sin starts—*a missing of a target*. At least that's the historical and biblical setting of the concept behind the word, sin.

Anytime I hear soldiers talking about sin, it is always with a different slant though. Sin has taken on more of a strictly religious taint than just this sense of missing the target. And that's because for most of us, sin is missing a *moral* target, an evil. And in Christian thinking, the moral targets are defined quite plainly in descriptions like murder, adultery, lust, envy, jealously, hatred and laziness—to name just a few interesting ones (there are other "little" sins, but nobody cares about the small stuff do they?). This is also one of the most curious words of the English language because of its intolerance. Sin, by definition, is a miss or failure that occurs and just is. It isn't a tendency or a mood. It is a failure to qualify in some sense to a standard, mostly referred to as moral, that is expected of me to perform. In this sense it is something I help to occur by making a decision about those standards and then failing. And when I fail, I commit an evil deed, and that evil deed or behavior is sin.

In the military you are expected to go to the range and qualify. If you fail to qualify, then that in the ancient Grecian term, is a *sin*. Maybe looking at sin this way is a new thing to you. At any rate, the key here is to understand the historical setting behind the theological word *sin*. I want you to understand that the bare essential idea of failure to meet a target is called sin, not that failing to qualify is "actually" a sin. Starting here will help clarify everything else we undertake in this Order. After all, from a theological perspective, this sort of thing doesn't change like the weather. Sin is going to always mean what it means whether we understand it that way for ourselves or not. In some sense this is a bias I have, but if you follow me, things will develop even further and you'll see what I mean. Keep reading.

Sin Can Be a Thing I Do

Another characteristic of sin as missing a target is that it isn't the same sort of failure for everyone. For instance, when you hear guys talk about sin, they usually talk about sexual sins. When you listen for women talking about sin, you don't hear anything. Women don't necessarily talk about specific sins and don't have the social need to. Men are more actual about their behavior and identify more quickly with the commission of evil deeds as being sin. Women on the other hand tend to dismiss that they might have performed any deeds that could be labeled evil. Maybe this has to do with the way we sexes view the world or something, but the fact is that men and women perceive sin quite differently from each other and it has much to do with our psychology and sense of behavior.

For instance, in church when you hear about sin, it is usually about some sort of sexual sin. And yet, the first sin articulated in Jewish tradition and history was in the Garden of Eden and it wasn't a sex sin, it was the sin of gaining unlawful power, the "knowledge of good and evil," something that Eve was convinced would bring both her and Adam into the power-zone in the Garden.[21] Even though Eve was naked at the time she was learning about the possibilities of this choice (and again the narrative pictures this story as a choice issue about sin), but this had nothing to do with nakedness. Nakedness was simply a fact of life for them. But the power was something they were lured into wanting by the serpent, mythologically representing Satan, the arch enemy of God. What he was doing and why he was there and the entire drama of the Garden is something to take up at another time.

In this garden setting, the woman is persuaded to go against the will of God and eat this fruit, which action would propel both her and Adam into a realization of good and evil, thus being like gods. Once they crossed the line and ate, they realized everything just as they were told, the nakedness became an issue, they were embarrassed and God was someone to be feared. And so with this comes the great story of the Fall of Man (man used generically) and the second and third interesting features of sin, that it is a choice made for the entire human race in this sense, and that men and women seem to have varying weaknesses and thus different types of sins. Men tend toward overt sins, easily identified, and women toward more complex, operational sin—hard to track and yet just as much missing the target as the overt sins of murder and fornication perhaps more commonly "associated" with men.

---

[21] The story line is that God had forbidden each of them to eat from the tree of the knowledge of good and evil. Once they had succumbed to the serpent's temptation, they were enlightened. But that enlightenment is not what God had in mind for them. That event, called the Fall in theological terms, becomes the origin of the sin of the entire human race so to speak. This is also considered what is called "original sin."

It appears when you're in church that only men really do the sinning because their sins are more easily identified with by the male clergy who figure that women are smart enough to grasp the gist of what is being said about sin so they emphasize the "male" sins as a rule. That's why sin in church is always called lust and adultery—traditionally men's sins. When lust is talked about it is usually a man lusting for a woman, and so my point—sin is basically male oriented because most ministers are male and tend to think of their own weaknesses rather than those of their congregation. And again, a sermon wouldn't have much punch if the minister or chaplain were to talk about manipulation, but that too could be a sin!

Like I said before, maybe men just need this sort of obvious approach about sin. However, women are in just as much need for clarification about sin, and so it doesn't hurt for them to realize that perhaps their tendencies to sin lie in the area of manipulation, envy, jealously, hatred, coveting, and so forth. If this does anything, it helps to situate our thinking about the traditional concept of sin. In both the male and the female, there are obvious ways of missing the target though the sins may not be as readily obvious.

Despite the male/female difference in "target failure" there is another distinction to sin that is basic—sin was generated as a choice by mankind and has affected all humankind in terms of an evil passed on to all. This is generally an accepted concept in the Christian and Jewish traditions and in the Islamic scriptures as well.[22] Once you move toward countries and religions of the East, the concept of sin disappears and has to be taught to be understood. Our Western concepts of missing the mark on the target are then based in this understanding that all people have judicially missed hitting the target because they are all descendants of Adam and Eve. Again, this is the concept which we call

---

[22] Abraham, the father of Jesus, Christians and Muslims alike, demonstrated a clear understanding of his need for propitation from sin when he builds and altar for sacrfice to God in Genesis 12 andd 22.

the Fall of Man. In this second main sense, *sin is an evil something that has judicial affects on us* whether we actually fail to hit a moral target or not, we are still affected by sin in the judicial sense. This is more the sense that we understand when we say that "ignorance of the law is no excuse" for breaking the law. The law still applies whether we realize it or not. This is the legal sense of sin. This is the other main and powerful concept of sin that we all live under.

Yet as this work has begun to illustrate, not everyone today has grown up in church or chapels and not everyone believes in sin either as an act of evil or a state of being evil.

For many people, sin in a "commercial" or "consumer" sense is a kind of goof-up, a problem, an accident, or something that gets in my way of doing what I want or need done. There's not so much a moral problem with sin, but a maturity problem. If there is any sin it is the sin of hurting oneself. So, it is like a tree down on the highway in front of me. And that illustration will work, so let's hold that idea too, and we will come back to the tree and see what to do with it in a minute. Most people agree that sin exists, but few agree as to what constitutes sin in either of the descriptions of it. Depending on your exposure to church, you are going to have varying ideas about what you consider sin to be. Maybe sin for you is just this aspect, a tree in your road.

Whatever picture works for you, sin is something that is part of who we are and has something to do with either our own moral failure or with things in life that aren't right. The result is often like the tree in the road blocking the way of my progress. In this sense, sin might possibly be eliminated with the right procedure or technique.

Whatever we finally determine is the "nature" of sin, whether an act of failure of some sort, or the condition of all humankind, or the unfortunate and distasteful events of life (tree in the road), it is sin that ultimately gets into our vocabulary as being the thing which complicates life and must be handled in some way or another for people to get along, for things to work better, and for me to feel in my heart that I'll be okay. For the truth of the matter is that sin often receives a lot of blame that doesn't belong to it, while people end up suffering endlessly from their suspicion about it.

ELUSIVE EFFECTS OF SIN

All religions have some sense of sin even if it is something of a sense of separation or lack of perfection. Eastern religions believe in a sort of sin in that we must appease ancestors for our personal failures and in another area of the East that we must die and hope to be reborn as a higher life-form due to our not being quite good enough yet. Whether the light from God you have[23] is from God as being "outside this world" and shining in over and on you (like the Western Christian sense) or whether you view God as being within your mind or in everything in the world (an Eastern sense), all the participants in most religions try to "do something" with sin and its effects.[24] This incidentally gives rise to the possibility of religion in cultures, as they attempted to devise ways of making themselves "right" with god. Later, I will ask you what you are doing to rid yourself of sin.

One of the things I see mostly in my work with military men and women is the tendency to demonize things that may not be

---

[23] This terminology "light that you have" is from the New Testament book of Romans chapters 1 and 2 where the Apostle Paul engages in a very interesting discussion about something called revelation. Bottom line is that God reveals himself to us all, somehow or some way. Each individual has some "light" according to the Apostle. We are only responsible for the "light" we have, either how bright or dim that light might be. Paul is worth reading, check him out.

[24] This idea is inherent in all forms of self-abnegation, denial or deprivation. Mankind always tends to view that getting to god is a process of getting rid of the bad kharma, or the things which distract me from god or gods, or paying for or being forgiven of the sins of which I am guilty. In effect human beings tend to like to isolate the feature of themselves that doesn't want to go along with god and call that part sin. In the most religious sense of that word the sin is something like murder. In the least religious sense of the word that is something like a tree in the road. In both cases people want and need to do something with it.

inherently "sinful," but because of the way they are trained, they tend to function better when they see the thing called "sin" outside of themselves. Maybe it is the way we are trained that makes us quick to try this, but it is very popular in the military to point to something or someone and call that bad, or sin, or the problem, and not identify anything that is closer to myself. This comes from assumptions made about the nature of man in general that we are basically good rather than that we are basically evil. All goes back to that Fall concept I spoke of earlier.

In most military marriages for example, sins usually surface as adultery. Guys and women, run out and have an affair with someone and then come seeking help with the effects of this sin. Usually, because the couple doesn't understand any more about sin than that this event occurred and it is sin, they never come to grips with the real sin in the marriage which might be issues of trust, expectations, role confusion, and maturity issues—where sin can lurk and mask itself in an event rather than be seen in someone's nature.

In other instances, young soldiers I work with will get into trouble with command and be undergoing UCMJ action and view the thing that caught them as the "sin" that got them.[25] They never see the sin that is working its devastating work in their life which led to the trouble in the first place. It is my experience that the "presenting" thing is rarely the sin to notice. It might be sensational, like taking drugs, or sleeping with someone else's wife or husband; but the more devious sin is the sin that prompts an individual to err in the first place. The person who can identify that sin nature within them, and why that sin is being enabled within them, will be the one who can conquer it decisively.

Like a game of sleight of hand, we have to look beyond the things we think are sin in order to see the real energy of sin in our lives. A wave breaking on the shore-front is only the last

---

[25] UCMJ: Uniform Code of Military Justice, the body of laws which regulate and govern all individuals who enter the military—called by its acronym, "UCMJ."

most impressive display of energy—there was an event far far away in the ocean which prompted that wave and gave birth to it. Sin is identical for everyone. It isn't today's escapade that is the worst sin, it is something far away that led the individual to today, which is where they must look for help. Sin operates in the same way for everyone no matter how much moral aspect there is to it, it still functions on people in the same manner. It creates multiple problems if it isn't treated. And it can also blind a person to denial of their wrongdoings or their own devious actions. That can be a rather mundane or routine denial and it can be a rather horrific wrongdoing as well.

Years ago a sharp ex-military guy named Brad entered the Bible college where I was attending. He was a good looking and intelligent young guy and was pretty popular with most everyone on campus. He had become a Christian in the Air Force and while on active duty had worked with a Christian para-church ministry that encouraged study and discipleship for Christians. It usually has a good effect on people. Brad was probably more disciplined than all the rest of us on campus and he became a model student. We knew each other but were not close friends. I do recall one night when I was cruising the dormitories talking to friends that I came upon Brad in his room with some other guys. He was sick and was asking God to heal him as he lay in his bed. I thought it somewhat humorous that he would simply just lie there and wait for healing and asked him why he didn't just get up and take some medicine. My comments weren't very well received by some of my pious fellow students in that room. We parted company that night and I didn't think any more about our exchange. Years later after we had all gone our separate ways I heard a grisly news report from graduates who lived in the community near the school where Brad was living while working and waiting on a missionary assignment. Brad had been arrested at his trailer for the murder of his baby, whom he had stabbed some eighteen times in the chest. Apparently he had been attending a Bible study of some sort and got the impression that his child was evil. He made his way home that evening with his wife, grabbed a knife and told his wife the child must die. His wife was assaulted while Brad jabbed the knife into his infant child. Brad was hauled off to jail and then was sentenced to prison for murder, later being released to the custody of his parents due to his deteriorating physical and mental condition. Brad eventually died of natural causes related to his mental delirium and deterioration. Brad is the extreme but authentic example of how sin can work its poison on even a good and disciplined mind.

Why Brad had determined that there was something evil in his child which warranted that child's death is something a court cannot decide. Yet, I wonder why Brad even began to think his child could have been so evil that he would have had to become an executioner. Where was the connection he had made about sin? And why did he assume that this evil was outside himself? Why didn't he question himself first? And why didn't he question the intensity with which he was pursuing this spiritualization of everything? At the point he was at, this over-spiritualizing of everything, very similar to the incident in the dormitory room, had become his sin. Spirituality at this intensity became unruly and a sin for Brad, but he couldn't see it.

This sad story illustrates in vivid detail what I'm saying about most people's impressions about sin and evil—they get the wrong idea and pursue the wrong fixes. Brad probably didn't need another Bible study as much as he needed to find out why he felt he was under such pressure to "act out" the impressions he thought were God's voice to him. I get worried when people in the service start taking God this seriously. It ought to signal to anyone that things are a little bit too intense. Watch out if you're in this category. Once you get "out there" this far, it is very difficult to come back and real tough to be rational any longer.

It isn't too different with the effects of sin. Whenever I listen to a soldier tearfully explain to me why he or she committed an unlawful act for which they are being punished, I always ask them why they did it. Maybe if they'd look at the cause and effect of decisions and relationships long before making their bad choice they would come upon some of the driving forces that work havoc in their life. But usually, people refuse to be rational when it comes to religion and rarely will anyone admit they went "overboard" on spirituality. Can you goof up with spiritual things? Yes.

But in another sense the story about Brad illustrates another point. Many religious people in the service get blindsided about the real issues they ought to be thinking about and chase issues and problems that don't need resolution today. It is often the case as I said before that religious soldiers will look away from themselves to things they believe are pushing them to sin when instead they should be looking at their own development. How you look at sin and how you understand it for your life makes tremendous differences in how you are going to live, work and make your way in the world.

EVIL THINGS HAPPEN

Sin isn't irrelevant. It plays some sort of role with each of us whether in our minds, lives, or in the events and people around us. About the time when you might think human nature is a wonderfully blessed thing, you hear about a horrible evil action that again reminds you of the sinfulness (evil) of mankind. And sin isn't just the stuff of terrorists. Sin is a like a strain of moral failure that exists in the fabric of human nature and lives there like an immune virus. And like an immune virus, you can treat its symptoms but unless you have access to a cure, it never quite goes away though it might disappear for periods of time.

This has a lot to do with the way I view the world to talk about sin this way. I admit that I am biased to see things in a Christian way. The Christian worldview, which borrows most all of its cosmology from the Jewish scriptures and traditions while energizing it with the dynamic of the resurrection hope of Jesus, has an answer for the sin problem. That answer is twofold: 1) Sin must be validated by us, and 2) it eventually must be destroyed or at least rendered ineffective.

It must be validated in the sense that you must somehow begin to understand that it is at work in you and in the world. That basic premise is a starting point for a Christian anthropology that makes sense of how evil works in the world. It has been part of systematic theology since the first century as the church fathers set out to codify the things they were certain of in terms of the teachings of the scriptures. The essential sinfulness of man based on the Fall event became a core doctrine to believe. Sin operates in human beings. If you do not recognize this then you must somehow account for evil in some way. Christian theology does it by recognizing the presence of sin in the human race.

My mother's mantra, "Some people are no damn good" is not a dislike of people but a recognition that sin has fully embedded itself in most people to the degree that they don't realize it is ruining their functionality with others around them. So many times in the service, junior enlisted members run into this type of person, a senior sergeant or petty officer whose entire life mission seems to be the harassment and blockade of others. It is almost as if because things didn't go right with them, they're going to make life a living hell for everyone else under their authority. These are the kind of people who have allowed the evil of sin to pollute their personalities and work ethic to the point that their life consists of one successive barrage after another of their "way of doing things" until people begin to seriously wonder whether they have any nice bone in their body at all.

I've seen the opposite too. Individuals who find a niche in the service somewhere and quietly ride out their paychecks not wanting to get involved with the difficulties of people's lives and problems. These are the people who seem to do nothing in our governmental offices, at least nothing anyone can put a finger to and verify. Where does such apathy come from? The same sinful nature that generates hatred generates laziness and carelessness. I run into this trait many times as I try to help people, and I find other people in the military system who hold up paperwork for small incidental items. Rather than call and set things right quickly, they toss the paperwork into a distribution basket, which returns the documents for a typo or a block to be checked. This holds up actions for people and causes many subsequent effects not the least of which is that military families suffer from careless administrative actions. People have to care about people in order to make this world a better place. This is one of the devious ways sin infects our systems and causes harm to others. And you thought this was going to be like *Exorcist III*! No, it isn't the wild demonic tales of sin that are the worst in my thinking, but the quiet and hidden ones people execute on others that are the most insidious.

Sin's character is insidious. And it is everywhere. In this sense, sin must be validated or recognized. We must be aware that it is ever with us in our world and in all the things we do. I've just noted a couple of seemingly benign instances in order to illustrate this. Another couple of books that talk about the character of sin from interesting perspectives are *The Great Divorce* and *The Screwtape Letters*, both by C.S. Lewis. Cleverly written pieces, these books are a journey for anyone who likes to think about these aspects of sin in a more sophisticated way.[26] If you want to know more about the way the Devil operates on a common individual you have to read *The Screwtape Letters*. Much of our focus on sin and evil deals so much with

---

[26] Of course most people are sold on the Hollywood concept of evil which is a Linda Blair type of head spinning, green vomit spitting, demonic terror instilling concept. Yet the Cambridge Professor of Classical Literature, C.S. Lewis spins the other side of the coin which is more insidious and probably more believable which is that the devil often works slowly for a lifetime on individuals to persuade them to ditch their faith in exchange for the niceities of life which can never save their souls in the long run.

the sensational while these books illustrate that the most devious operations are covert.

A further emphasis about validating sin is that you will never get rid of it. Once you admit it is part of you and your world, you must also realize that it never goes away and you never really shake it off. You are always subject to it, but you don't have to obey its urges. Nonetheless, it is part of the entire human condition. As a Lutheran, I also have some remedies for this, but I'll take those up in this second aspect of sin. Where I'm going with this is that sin doesn't have to be the thing that cripples you. You don't need to think that because sin is all around that this counterbalances all the good in the world. And further it doesn't mean that you are a lost cause either.

SIN OPERATES IN ME DESPITE ME

Sin is just a fact of life for those of us who are human and fallen creatures. We live in this natural sinful condition and have to get revisionary work done on our hearts before we can truly counter the effects of sin and the evil in the world. But given this fact, how do we proceed to the second sense of sin, that it is something inherently causing us to be sinful creatures?

Sin has to be destroyed. Its resistance to human-generated goodness is without par in the world. Yet it has to receive a death blow in order for us to truly subdue its effect in the world. The best we can do with sin is give it a declaration though. Sin doesn't really have any power since the resurrection of Jesus. That event broke Satan's power to unlimited human resources and rendered sins only as powerful as people will allow them to be. In the Christian sense, this power was broken by the sacrifice of Jesus Christ being the sinful requirement of our sins. No other incident in history has had more impact than this, that Jesus Christ laid down his life for his friends. And he mentioned that this was the most honorable thing anyone could do for their friends. The "cross event," as it is commonly referred to, is the thing that broke all that judicial power of sin[27] and now renders it as harmless as a church mouse.

Now none of this guarantees that you will be a nicer or better person, but it should suddenly provide you with a way of making sense out of sin in the world and the sin that lives in you as a human being in this sinful world.

Once we acknowledge sin is in us and all around us and that we are very vulnerable, and that it can be rendered powerless, we are a bit closer to getting a firm grip on the concept of salvation and how someone paying for your sins makes sense. Here I confess I am thoroughly Christian because this is the stuff that identifies Christianity most clearly. And because this is unique, it ought to be your starting place for spiritual orientation rather than a falling-off place.

Oftentimes, I hear soldiers speaking with what seems authority about God, human salvation and life in the world, like philosophers or theologians without a license to practice. And there is a tendency in this current postmodern age to claim that the ideas that surface are not just right, they are original. I call this tendency the "uniqueness of triviality" and it is rampant in our services today.

Much Ado about Nothing

Shakespeare's play bears the best description of the current philosophic and theological sickness in the ranks of service personnel. The uniqueness of triviality finds young people espousing their views of many things, including sin, and reducing the

---

[27] This statement is loaded with theological implications that I don't have time here to entertain. Simply put I'm referring to the exhaustive theological doctrines of justification and redemption, which if you wish to read about can be found in the writings of St. Augustine, Martin Luther, Jean Calvin, the Westminster Divines, etc. When I use the word *judicial*, I'm referring to the power of the event of the Cross which legally satisfied the demands of sin for each of us in the vicarious death and resurrection of Jesus Christ. This is bedrock Christian theology for Protestants, Catholics, and most people who believe in the Christian tradition.

ideas to assumptions without basis. If you read this chapter and you then turn around and suggest that sin is nothing but a whimsical thought, then you must also find the basis that should affirm your position. In my argument I suggest that my ideas are Christian in nature. Yet, today, ideas are floating around that are "deconstructing" concepts like this one on sin into one-dimen-

sional expressions without basis in history or thought.

To a degree, everyone is entitled to their opinions about sin, but because it is such a powerful ingredient in the human condition, I prefer to make sure that it doesn't come under the fire of this triviality. We can function with sin in the world but we cannot properly understand *Under Orders* if anyone's opinion can dismiss sin away with a "whatever." Somewhere, in your thinking process you must determine the values you will strike into stone and you must engrave this one carefully. To reduce it away with whimsical irrelevance will be to attempt to describe Hawaii without palm trees and hula girls. Deep inside the human condition is nested this tendency to miss the moral target time and time again. Without some sort of realization and remedy, sin continues its work unhindered, and you will end up missing the moral target every time you try.

Christianity does something about sin's power but doesn't take it away completely. Other religions may have you strive or deny yourself in order to achieve another level of realization. Yet Christianity has this purging quality to it that strikes deep into the power of sin and renders it ineffective. Ineffective in a couple of ways.

Sin becomes ineffective to be your only moral choice. As a human being you have a choice to be part of the social answer rather than the social problem. When I don't recognize that I'm running only on sin's capabilities, I never have access to options for myself. Only my good natured-ness can help me contribute to the betterment of my unit or team. When I realize that sin is an agent, I can more quickly identify my own tendency to corrupt a group and bring havoc to what needs cohesion and team confidence. My sin can also make my agenda more important than my unit's agenda and thus lead to unit failure.

When I don't have any way of striking at sin's power, I will always find myself rather gutless to kill the power of sin's influence in my life. I'll feel disempowered against it because I am without power against it.

A young Specialist in the Army years ago couldn't find it within himself to work with his young wife and child. He had had an affair with a senior officer's daughter and his unchecked passions had led to the disruption of his marriage and the heartbreak of his beautiful wife. Things got even worse when he took out his anger on her and beat her. If you had looked at him you'd have thought he had just stepped off of a *Family Ties* rerun. His uniform was impeccable and he never missed his formations. But the day he met with me and his wife, she pulled back her blonde hair to reveal a bloody scrape behind her ear put there in his anger to keep her quiet about everything. All she wanted was his love, affection and commitment. Not even their toddler warmed his heart. He just had to divorce her. If he had only been able to accommodate the idea that sin was operating in his relationship he would have at least had an approach to his problem. He could have realized too that sin was operating deep within him to cheat him of his life by making his obvious lusts more important that his real loves. He fell prey like all the rest to his own trivial assessment of life and marriage. In this situation he was fooled about his affections thinking that the officer's daughter was the "right" person for him. He didn't look deep within at the sin which was short-circuiting his own decision making process. He burned out his moral logic. He goofed up. He broke apart a great family.

But he's just one of many. Basic error was not seeing that the evident culprit was not how much the officer's daughter wanted to have sex with him, but not realizing that he had a fundamental malfunction as a result of sin. Sin would always draw him from the things he loved to things he wanted instead. A simple formula. He just couldn't get it.

He had a moral choice but he was tricked by sin into thinking he could only do one thing and that was the wrong thing. The funny thing is that everyone has their opinions on religion, but few people have any idea how to fight this "shadow war" on sin.

Sin's capabilities are much stronger than supposed by people and much trickier than supposed. In *The Screwtape Letters*, the senior devil, Uncle Wormwood, counsels the young devil, Screwtape, to not give up on his victim because over a lifetime, he will be successful as a devil if the man thinks the greatest evil is that he would get drunk or cheat on his wife or murder someone. Because if he thinks this way, he will perhaps try to live a good life by not doing those things called "sin." But in reality the greatest evil that Screwtape could have him commit is that the man would simply not care about his essential sinfulness and seek the remedy for it.

considerations

Consideration 1: What is sin? The most important question you will ever ask and seek an answer to. Remember that it is both an action and a condition. One causes the other. It might not be politically correct to talk about sin, there has to be some word that expresses this condition. Go back to the *hamartia* example and study that concept and then look at the chapter in Romans written by the Apostle Paul. Try to connect the concepts. Examine yourself and determine how you fix this in your own mind.

Consideration 2: What is confession of sin? Some people go to a priest to confess their sins in hopes that by following the requirement to confess that the absolution from the priest will grant forgiveness. I think this confession can be good but it need not be limited to a confessional. Think about the idea of confession and ask yourself why it is important to "own up to" sin. Read more about this in the book of First John in the New Testament. There are some very positive aspects to confessing your sins to people. Yet you may also confess your sins to God directly.

Consideration 3: What do other people have to do with my sin? The Jewish concept of sin also included the horizontal relationship we have with people. There is no such thing as being "right with God" and wrong with people. I can't go hurt someone and then go to chapel and get religious and think that God respects that! Even Jesus expressed this Jewish concept in his saying, "Do unto others as you would have them do unto you" and when he said, "Whatever you do to others you do to me." Christianity is Jewish in nature and it follows the same structure of absolution—we must treat people well or we cannot be right with God.

ORDER EIGHT

Choose Your Profession—What am I doing here and where am I going?

"I'm going to live off my investments when I get out of the Army…"

an young infantry soldier

GETTING IN AND OUT OF THE SERVICE

I have a million stories like this one, but it had to be the funniest one I'd ever heard. A young soldier entered my office and haltingly began to fumble around at his concern—he wanted to get out of the military. He didn't look much more than maybe eighteen years old and his face still had the signs of being a teenager. He was discouraged with the way things were going in the unit and he didn't think he'd made the right choice about his life and joining the service. Haven't we all been there at some time in some way?

I sat patiently and listened to this soldier describe all the things he wanted to do when he got out of the service. His eyes were filled with anticipation as he described driving a truck, working for a friend and making a new start living off his investments and so forth. It all seemed so right to him. Then I asked him how much he earned every month. He made just under a thousand dollars a month—a great deal for a teenager who pays no lodging costs. Then I asked him how he would fund himself once he exited the service and he said he had some money saved up. (I once knew a sergeant who was independently wealthy and simply needed to go to work every day for something to do—this guy wasn't like the sergeant though.) Curiously, I then asked him what sort of investment fund he had that would enable him to live off of his investments—after all, he was very young! He told me he had about seventeen hundred dollars saved up. I stared at him and asked him how he'd live off that. He figured he could for a while. "Maybe a week," I said to him. I'm still smiling and shaking my head over that conversation.

I never cease to be amazed at the creativity of some of the people who walk into my office! I have to confess that his answer still makes me smile—I hope he has revised his plans. I recommended that he hang around and build that fund before getting out of the military. I don't really recall what he ended up doing though.

I think military service is a great thing for everybody. It builds confidence and helps young people understand the requirements of an adult world within the safety net of an organization that helps them accomplish their short-term goals. Those of us in the service have a great benefit to be able to participate in a government organization and learn so many things at all levels of service within it.

But for many service members, there are problems with both entering the service and problems in getting out of it. The life of a soldier or sailor is complicated at many turns by the temporal nature of living a life in uniform. And it is further complicated when that tour of duty is finally over and we have to "go back" to the civilian world and get used to an entirely different system of doing things. One of the most difficult things is to watch a uniformed individual leave the "system" and return to the civilian world. It is probably as scary as the young person who entered service life, like so many, scared and intimidated, only to realize that they could conquer the training and service with pride. All of us face this common challenge of the profession we embrace, whether as a private or as a professional career officer.

As this book is for those who have entered the service, I assume that you probably are making your journey through an assignment during some pretty challenging times. Most everyone in the service is being affected by the war on terrorism in various ways. Not only are most families in the U.S. affected by having at least some of their family members in the military, but most of the people in the military are deploying in support of an operation either to Iraq, or Afghanistan, or Kuwait, or South America, or Korea or the Philippines, just to name the obvious places. Many other locations are classified where we have people stationed performing sometimes mundane and other times heroic efforts for peace and stability.

One of the most common problems service members face is the challenge of the profession to which they have been called. Everyone comes to the military for something. In exchange for their commitment, the service pays them, rewards them with educational benefits, provides free asistance of every variety, houses them and then if they stay long enough will reward them with increased rank and eventual retirement. The military is what we call a "time-honored profession." It is that not only for the generals but for the privates as well. It can be a tough profession for all ranks though. The inherent problems of service life are little to be compared with the problems that come later. For the service has that "protective" quality so that you always know certain things will be in place. You can expect there to be a formation for accountability, you can expect to have to put on your uniform every day, and you can anticipate you will be on duty over the weekend sometimes!

And these inconveniences of service life come to an end for each of us. Finally, we exit the service and we face a question that we must answer, what will I do with my life and what will I accomplish?

This is what we call profession or calling. In the Christian sense, God calls us to various ways of serving in this life. The service again is one of the best organizations in the world for helping young people and older ones as well recognize that there are some things more valuable than cash flow—things like integrity, courage and commitment. In the service we find our cohesion based on those things. Those are essential to winning in combat.

In talking with the soldiers I work with, fear of the future and my role in the future is one of the number one concerns of young people in uniform. Years ago it might not have been as threatening an issue. After the Vietnam war, the US went into a period of relative ease. Despite the oil crisis in the mid 70s, you could pretty much depend on a growing economy and pursuing your lifestyle and interests. The US has always enjoyed this burgeoning prosperity. It also exists in other places in the world like in Europe, but not to the extent and way it does in America. America is protected by a great deal of ocean and has neighbors in the north and south with which it is friendly. So if you are living in the US today you don't have as many concerns as everyone else. Yet, there are real concerns today that didn't even exist in 1970.

One of the most remarkable features of today's world is that service members are the central effort in the war on terrorism, and that war is shaping our destiny. Along with that, soldiers and sailors, marines and airmen find themselves faced with dangerous missions today like they never have before. For the first time since Vietnam and the Gulf War, the Coast Guard is deploying to the Near East. Everyone is involved including National Guard soldiers at home and serving in rotations abroad. Some of the easy decisions are not so easy anymore. This war is raising concern levels because it is touching everyone and pushing them out to foreign soil. Futures are filled with images of combat and weapons of mass destruction. Images of what that might mean are part what of every service members fears.

The decision to enter the military is now more complicated than ever. Whether you are a strapping farm boy from Keokuk, Iowa or a whisper of a young girl from San Bernardino, California entering the service today, you might end up in Kazakhstan in six months or cruising the Mediterranean aboard a carrier with five thousand of your closest friends. Military service today comes with the certain promise of deploying to hostile fire zones. And there is no sign that this will change in the near term.

Two questions have to be answered by every service member these days: First, what in the world were you thinking when you joined the service? And second, what will you do when you get out? In between those questions come a great deal of problems and wavering. I hope that if you are between those questions that you will find your way here and settle yourself with the good choice you've made.

A SOUND DECISION

The service was a good decision. No matter how things work or where you go, you made a great decision. Service for country is noble, it is time honored, and no one can take it from you. Few people get to actually "serve" their country. When you have the chance you should do so proudly. Our country and our life, its freedoms and its privileges are the result of many people before you who have served their country too. You must believe in your decision and not question it. Part of being a professional in uniform is believing in the obligation of service. I'm not saying this as a spokesman for the military but as a professional myself. For even a chaplain chooses to enter the military. We enter the military just like everyone else and raise our hand just like you did in basic training, promising "to defend the Constitution of the United States against all enemies, foreign and domestic." Military service since classical days has always been a noble profession. It is always good, regardless of whether some days you'd just like to walk away. Stick with it. You get more from this experience than the institution does. I have rarely ever heard an older person regret military service; in fact, I cannot remember anyone saying that.

Standing in the checkout line at a military quick-stop store the other day, I listened to a couple of individuals talk about their current jobs. The guy behind the counter shook his head and said he wished he was still in the service, to which the other fellow behind me said, "Everyone thinks how great it will be when they retire but they just have no idea. The twenty years I spent in the service was the greatest time of my life." I watched and listened to these two guys talk for a few minutes and tried to soak up the optimism because on any given day I too can feel like my job really sucks. But then I realize that it is service, not entertainment. And it makes sense to serve.

There have always been times when military service wasn't so great, but there has never been a time when those who served weren't doing the best they could for their country. I recall the tough days of the late 60s when all of us guys thought we'd do a tour in Vietnam and perhaps never come back home. Our country was locked in a fierce conflict with a tenacious enemy who survived our napalm and our carpet bombs. We eventually withdrew from that conflict and based much of our common sense in combat upon its lessons. Yet the soldiers who served then were no less noble than you now. The position of the country or the politics does not have to interfere with your commitment. Your choice to serve is yours.

And this is really what I mean when I speak about the calling to your profession. You make your choices but there are higher things than your oath that hold you in place. You are part of a great tradition and a noble profession. Yet too, God is in the process and the product you are experiencing.

SOMEONE IS WATCHING OVER ME

The current war on terrorism has brought a certain focus on the religion of Islam, highlighting the consciousness of God that Islamic faithful exhibit. Often on news programs you will see special reports showing Islamic faithful kneeling and praying toward Mecca. We are sometimes given the impression that Muslim faithful are more religious than Christians. The Muslim extremist party line that all Americans are infidels is truly sad and false. After all, one of the central reasons people came to the New World was for religious freedom of worship, which had been denied them in England. Today, Americans are no different than anyone else, for even the Muslim nations do not all stop what they are doing to bow in prayer time give times a day. It goes on around them just like church goes on around Americans. However, the war has brought this renewed focus on religious practice, the presence of God and the place of religion in everyday human lives.

It is probably one of the best things you can do to find God in your life and work. One of the most consistent things which "postmodern" people are interested in is relevancy of their lives and work. People want to know that who they are in the world is significant and that what they do is meaningful.

Yet it is tough to find the meaning sometimes. One of my nephews served on the USS *Constellation*, affectionately called "Connie" by the crew, before it was decommissioned on August 7, 2003. He lived in a tight bunk area with his other shipmates and called his living room that tight eighteen inches of headspace over his mattress. His clothes and personal effects fit underneath the mattress and in a small wall locker. If he wasn't working then he was sleeping. Eating cannot be leisure aboard an aircraft carrier. Free time is limited. You see the same people on your shift every time you pull that shift. Like Bill Murray in *Groundhog Day*, this young sailor fits into his world and finds his way. What are the elements that help him find meaning in that? How many sailors can be recruited by offering high school seniors eighteen inches of headspace for six months at a time?

The answers depend on yourself and how you understand you within your world.

GUIDELINES FOR LIVING IN A SMALL WORLD

In the Old Testament, there is a story about someone named Joseph. We find Joseph isolated from his family who live in Israel. Joseph's brothers had jacked him up by selling him to slave traders. Joseph finds himself in jail on trumped up charges and it looks as if there is no way out for him. People he thought were his friends had promised to put in a good word on his behalf to try to get him out of jail, but no one remembered to carry through with their promise, and Joseph was left to rot in jail. Sometimes the military is like that for service people, and sometimes people start to really rot personally, spiritually and emotionally. Joseph decided to keep his Jewish faith, decided to hang tough despite the "sell-outs" who had left jail.

Came to be in the story that God gave Joseph the same dream the Pharaoh dreamed and soon Joseph was out of jail and advising the King of Egypt.[28] You could say it was timing or being in the right place at the right time. And, you could say it was God. What is important to keep in mind is that Joseph didn't see it as his part in life to rot in the circumstance he was thrust into during that time. He maintained his faith, he kept his vision, and he didn't get bitter.

---

[28] This is a classic story in Genesis worth reading. It has all the subtleties and currents of a great story: the youngest child, the animosity of brothers, the love of a father despite all odds, the lure of sexual favors from a powerful woman, the courage to hold to one's beliefs despite pressure, being imprisoned under false charges, being exonerated due to your spiritual capabilities, leading and managing a powerful country, the protection of your own country and family, and unlimited and unconditional forgiveness for crimes committed against an innocent brother.

Seems with the operational tempo of the military today, that it is critically important for airmen, marines and soldiers to keep their head in their spiritual game.

Five rules for living in a small world:

Rule 1: See the end from the beginning. Keep in mind what you are after and how much you want that thing. To do that you have to visualize stuff. You have to keep that vision in front of you as your goal every day. The grueling repetitive nature of military life means that there won't be any time for you to stop and think about all these sublime things. You're going to have to write down your goal and live every day for it. This isn't the end of your life, it's only a few years of time. Remember the choices you make here, either for good or for error, will require either payment or will pay you when it is over. Don't be foolish about your choices.

Rule 2: Be passionate about your life. I don't mean sexually, I mean believe in yourself and where you are headed. Joseph was really energized, the same concept, about his life so that even when he was in jail he was still motivated to keep going. If you don't believe in yourself, you're going to be a quick target for discouragement. Don't sell yourself out cheaply for sexual favors or be quick to give up on what you were trained to believe and know. Bring your life to the service and make the service better for it. Physical passion is short-lived. Living passionately for your life brings you into a meaningful responsibility with yourself.

Rule 3: Nothing lasts forever. There is an end and it comes about sooner or later. When the training is tough and relentless, you have to turn back and remember this, you have to, to be successful. Persistence grows out of your understanding of this fact. When you are in your early 20s, it seems like waiting until the weekend is like waiting forever. As you grow older you realize it isn't. This thing of the different perceptions of time is very complicated, and I cannot explain it. All I can do is tell you to keep this rule in mind and your enlistment in the military will work out just fine.

Rule 4: Center yourself spiritually. Find a time and place where it is just you and God, make that rendezvous your religious habit and keep it. Great things don't need a great cathedral to work. The greatest times with God come in the tightest places, the smallest bunk areas, finding a moment or two to listen to God or to talk to God. Chapel can be that place too, but many people just aren't able either to go to chapel at the posted time, or they don't feel they are accustomed to that experience. But everyone has a private time alone, time to read a scripture, to whisper a prayer. Find it.

Rule 5: Be yourself. Even with all the limitations of the military lifestyle, the uniform, the protocols, remember to be true to yourself every day. The military needs your input. Don't copy someone else, but be yourself. Yet use this time to develop too. Many times your leaders will point out to you things that you need to work on. This is a great time to do that. Remember, this gives you the time to work on relationships, authority and consistency of character. Be you, and learn to make yourself better during this time capsule of your life. Remember, many people change once they enter the military because they meet up with so many different individuals. Many wish they had never lost themselves after it is all over. Start right, stay you.

LIVING IN A LAND FAR, FAR AWAY

Current military operations throughout the world are making a generation of young people head out into the desert and onto the ocean for what seems like endless months of uncertainty.

Civilians at home cannot begin to understand this sort of employment. It takes a toll on people to live separated from their spouses and children and the familiar things of home. Like no other profession, the military service is a profession that doesn't accept misbehavior and refuses to give in to personal choices.

Once deployed, service members seem to run into these human pitfalls early on. It isn't a normal thing for people to live like this, to have to make a living based on the possibility of war. Yet it is our business. And we do it pretty well. However I have found that the journey out to this world and back can be filled with hazards.

Relationships in the workplace are a problem for everyone. In the military, it is even more complex. Deployed far away from home in an institution that doesn't recognize male or female except for bath and wash areas, the moral distinctions begin to blur. You can find yourself talking about things in a land far away that you'd never talk about if you worked at the local bank downtown. It is easier to treat human sexuality in terms of sport rather than as intimacy. It is easier to diminish the relationship of that person in the photo in your locker once confronted by the intensity of a passionate relationship with a fellow uniformed body right in front of you. The lines of behavior begin to blur. It requires a tenacious and determined person to find their way through this maze of hazards.

Following the five rules above will help keep you focused and directioned (a word I've coined). In addition, you might also remember that "someone is watching over you." Let's go back to the opening part of this chapter where I mentioned that God is in our lives whether we realize it or not.

People can think that they live completely autonomously, that is, that there is no God and that everything that happens happens because of chance and by virtue of our own strength. And though there is a great deal that I would agree with in terms of the choices you make in life (well, even the five rules in this chapter have to do with you making decisions, don't they?), there is another part of life that I do not believe we can control and that is the "over watch" that God provides to each one of us whether we are Christian or Muslim, Jewish or Pantheistic. A Jewish friend once explained to me the concept of God watching over us in terms of his purpose for our lives. As a Christian, I believe that whether you are the Admiral of the Fleet or you are a private working on a Marine Landing Force ship, God does over-watch of you and your life.

This doesn't mean that nothing will ever harm you but it does mean that every life is sacred and priceless. Even as every member of the crew facilitates the operations of the ship, every life has this incredible essential value, just because you are a human being. It is part of Jewish thought and Christian thought that God sees and cares for each person. And God does care about the future, your future. And yet maybe God cares about it a bit differently than you do. Whereas you might think about it in terms of cash flow, investments, cars and great employment, I don't think any of those things ultimately define a worthy profession or life.

Each individual has a purpose, a role, a place. And even if that place is simple and common, it is still a sacred place. One of the infectious problems that permeates current thinking amongst many people is that unless I make a certain amount of money every month, or drive a particular automobile, that my life will not be as significant as someone else. My chaplain assistant during OIF, a senior NCO (E7), told me that one of the problems in the black military community today is the misconception that black service members have the feeling that they must "present" a look of wealth in order to fit into the current black culture expectation. Though he too is black, he doesn't measure his life like that and views education, family, marriage and accomplishments as more important than driving a new car. It takes a great deal of courage to understand that your personal worth and value doesn't have to come from what you are seen wearing or driving.

As our culture continues to define itself during this time of war and distress, there is still the strong possibility that American youth can graduate and pick and choose their lifestyle and living conditions, unlike other parts of the world. Outside of western Europe and North America, youth are limited by educational deprivations, cultural limitations, and geopolitical divisions, which dictate rather than permit people to aspire beyond their current situation. It has always been pretty much this way for American youth. And service youth at least get the opportunity to see this disparity first hand.

The measure of a person shouldn't be what they become, nor what they possess, but should be themselves. Like the old adage from Job says, "Naked we came into this life and naked we shall leave this life." So with such a future ahead of us, we should reconsider our function in the rat race of life. Reconsider our goals and expectations. This is why I believe so strongly in Being Yourself even when you are in the military.

Some may have the conception that the military restricts individuals from being unique—but that is only during basic training. Once you find your way into your unit, you can allow yourself to be who you are without the same restrictions. However, in doing so, remember that your goal should reflect your essential belief in who you are and what you bring to the unit regardless of rank and position.

ONE CHOICE WINS

I was training with a Light Infantry company of soldiers one day and had followed this platoon through an infiltration towards an objective. The enemy shot at us and we returned fire to suppress them. During the firefight (with blank ammo), some smoke canisters were thrown to mask the movement of our flanking squads. The grass caught fire and there was total mayhem with the smoke, the fire, the coughing, yelling and the crack of M-16s and machine guns pumping imaginary bullets through the haze. In the midst of the firefight the lieutenant was shot and killed (again a war game) and his radio operator (RTO) had also gone down. The radio crackled as the company commander attempted to gain a visual picture of the battle. Few soldiers remained alive. Yet one specialist (E4, we call them), heard the radio and crawled over and began giving the commander a view of the battle situation. The small remaining soldiers regrouped and fought their way to victory as the commander brought in close air support to kill the enemy assault.

Later that afternoon the platoon was gathered together in the hot sun along with the then Chief of Staff of the Army, General Gordon Sullivan, for an after action review (AAR) of the firefight. General Sullivan listened patiently for the AAR to get to a certain point and then interrupted it. He called for the E4 who had grabbed the radio through the smoke and fire of the assault area. The soldier raised his hand not knowing what was to follow. The general then quizzed him on his actions and the soldier forthrightly answered each question. Then General Sullivan said, "I want everyone here to know that what this young soldier did here today by performing that simple act of grabbing the radio is what wins battles." His calmness of mind and his training clicked in at just the right time and enabled him to save the rest of his platoon. Without his action, this platoon would have all died in the hot sun today. He then handed the young soldier a general's coin and a pocket knife and saluted the E4 and thanked him.

Rank doesn't matter as much as role. That we perform our duty well and conscientiously is all part of understanding how and where we fit into this life with meaning. Many of you reading this are often troubled by the temporary hassles that come along with serving in the military, but those come and go. My challenge to you is to look beyond the little stuff to the simple role you play in the military. Understand how big it is in reality. When the USS *Cole* was hit that day several years ago, nobody cared about rank in the fire and the chaos of the strike. They jumped into the burning hulk to do the simple things they had been trained to do. Sailors performed basic procedures of fire-fighting and rescue and made a significant difference in the losses that day because they focused on the significance of their contribution under fire.

Don't ever lose sight of the importance of yourself in the grand scheme of things. This chapter has been all about the profession you're in and the one you are going to. The one ahead is simple compared to this. Most people who exit the military always look back with fond appreciation at the training and development they experienced in the military. The future is made today.

You determine today what tomorrow will be and bring by beginning today to put into practice the simple things I've been talking about. One of my colleagues at the Chaplain Center and School jokingly told me that life is what happens to us between meet-ings—we had so many of them! Truth is that life for most service members is what happens when you're caught up in the middle of your stress about tomorrow. Make it your ambition to work today on finding your niche in the unit and performing your tasks to the best of your capabilities. Don't talk like the young soldier at the outset of this chapter who told me all about the terrific things he would do as soon as he exited the military. Begin today to work on the five rules that can make you effective today in your unit and can bring you a sense of personal fulfillment.

During the Mogadishu nightmare we have come to know as "BlackHawk Down," Sgt. Streucker told another soldier to clean out the back of the HMMWV vehicle. A dead soldier's body parts were scattered around in it. The soldier stood petrified at the sight. Sgt. Streucker dove into the task and did it himself. He knew there was little use in thinking about the situation, that if other soldiers were to live, he would have to get this done quickly. Sgt. Streucker didn't have time then to think about the fact that one day he would be an army chaplain serving on active duty as he is.[29] That moment and that time demanded his attention and service. For you it is no different. Your contributions, which you may think small and unnoticed, are all part of a greater organization that depends on every individual performing as a unit to accomplish the mission. Your choice matters. Many of the seemingly unmeaningful tasks you are ordered to perform today build something deeper and more meaningful in you for tomorrow. Your toughest job will be to look beyond today to that tomorrow.

considerations

Consideration 1: How can you understand your job in the military as a calling? The idea of calling is a biblical concept that means that what you are doing is both something worthwhile and something you believe God is involved in. Think about the reasons that made you join the service and then think about where you are now.

---

[29] Sgt. Streucker has become Chaplain (Captain) Streucker and serves with the 82nd Airborne Division now. I met him while working as the Officer Training Analyst at the U.S. Army Chaplain Center and School at Ft. Jackson, SC. He is one of the most settled, normal and balanced individuals I have ever met. A remarkable chaplain.

How far apart are those? Can you reinvent your enlistment? Can you re-energize your life today by realizing your profession in the military has a "call" aspect to it?

Consideration 2: When your life in the military begins to look dismal what do you use to fix that? Look into the book of Genesis and read the story of Joseph and his family. Many times when we think our life "sucks" God is actually actively involved in it. Like many mystery movies, it depends on your perspective as to the "suck" factor. Investigate how the Joseph story can relate to your military experience today. Look over my Five Rules for Living in a Small World and see if those can help you "re-picture" your own life in your small world. Remember your disposition in this postmodern way of thinking is that things have to occur right now. God's timing is often lengthy and doesn't have the same demand for instantaneous correction.

Consideration 3: What is the value of a human life like yours? In order to answer this effectively, I think you have to determine what your value system is to make an informed decision about yourself. What are the things you value? Once you determine that you will know quickly what your life is worth. Perhaps it is a dollar amount. Or perhaps, your life is priceless. Remember the most precious things in life cannot be purchased.

ORDER NINE

How do I understand where to begin with faith and who knows what is valid?

"I will tell you...how hard or rather impossible is the attainment of any certainty about questions such as these in the present life."

Simmias to Socrates in the dialogue, "Phaedo"

NOT A RIGHT DAY

My oldest son, a Marine Lieutenant serving in the Infantry,[30] as a child used a curious expression from the first time he uttered it, "This is not a right day!" He would turn around to me and declare this like a little all-knowing Jedi or something. It was both curious and alarming. It made me wonder if I had the next Dhali Lama on my hands or a dark comic! Turns out after all these years that he is extremely intuitive by nature and seems to know when things

---

[30] As I wrote this my son was a Platoon Leader with Echo Company, 3rd Platoon, the 2nd Battalion of the 1st Marine Division, 15th Marine Expeditionary Unit, Special Operations Capable (MEUSOC) fighting in the city of Basra in Operation Iraqi Freedom. He went on a year later and served as Platoon Commander for Echo Company, Weapons, in Fallujah, Iraq in April 2004.

just aren't working right. But the words seem to ring true even today. Some things in life just aren't quite right. And it's often difficult to know what is just quite "right" in life sometimes.

For Western thinkers and peoples, being right, correct, is part and parcel of being good as well. Germans have a schoolhouse phrase teachers repeat from childhood, *"Was ist richtig ist wichtig, und was ist wichtig is richtig,"* i.e., "What is right is correct and what is correct is right." This suggests that rightness is based on correctness. Can that really be a true statement? If your criterion for rightness is correctness, I guess so. But ultimately it isn't a right statement. Something might be correct in procedure and wrong morally in content. Often what is right isn't correct to us because we don't see things the "right way"!

Being right has also become a highly charged issue in the world today as Islamic countries struggle to maintain the rightness of their religion in the face of Islamic extremists who franchise Islamic religion to promote their terror. The United Nations has taken up a position in this pursuit of "rightness" as it slowly processes complaints against worldwide terror while dragging its feet against swifter prosecution of countries that harbor terrorists. People in international studies and practice are substantially divided over rightness, much of it stemming from political positions but also religious points of view which drive politics. Israel and the Palestinians are locked in an unending fight over the rightness of their causes.

Being right is a big issue. This chapter doesn't seek to resolve the issue for politics or the current Islamic confusion. But for individual belief for the marine or soldier on the ground fighting for his or her country and for their understanding of meaningful faith in the midst of such confusion, what can be offered to help explain the puzzle? The current generation of military service members have the same personal needs to intellectually and spiritually understand and engage their faith as did their grandparents who never had to ask those questions from within a hostile fire zone. Today the urgency of understanding the powerful forces beneath the surface of our belief demands incisive and careful probing.

If we were to wait until everything was "quite right" we would probably wait a long, long time. When it comes to understanding how life fits together, I think it is even more true. There are many perspectives, ideas, thoughts and positions, and all of them have some truth to them. Yet somewhere we have to plant our flag of discovery and declare where we personally stand. Knowing enough to declare that is what this chapter is all about. Read further if you want to check your *weltanschauung* (German philosophical term for worldview) or way of looking at the world and where you fit into it. For eventually, how you view yourself and the world around you determines your decisions. And what if how you view things isn't right? Can it be that there is a right way?

This Ninth Order seems very appropriate to me because so many of the soldiers I meet are concerned about ultimate and right reality but don't know where to start looking for that reality. Orders Three and Four were concerned about Knowing God and somewhat about understanding how we might believe. However, at that time I chose not to get into what I want to talk about here. This chapter is all about the many philosophies that permeate the basis for the way we think and believe in our world. And without getting too deep into philosophy and interpretation, I want to show you "a way of thinking" which that work for you too. When you exit this working process you will have a grasp of your own situation better than you had when you entered it.

This chapter talks about all those curious and sometimes suspicious things you wonder about with regard to God, the Bible and believing. Most of the people I meet these days want their questions answered but few people are helping them out with their questions. I am going to engage here in some direct talk about all those sacred things you always wondered about and then I'm going to bring you back to where this all starts and show you how each one of you is ultimately the master of his or her own life. That is an awesome responsibility and true. It may not become as important how "right" you are about your religious views as how you approach your view and the views of others. In the last chapter of *Under Orders* I will pick up the issue of how all religions fit together and what seems to be an answer for us.

DECIDING WHAT TO BELIEVE

Who determines what you hold as a belief and who says it's right and true? That sounds like a Consideration for the end of the chapter but we need to tackle this stuff right here. For most of us, our conflicts are generated out of who we are, how we've been raised, and what we've come to believe about life—something "shaped" in us by our families and our experiences. But sometimes that stuff is bigger than we are and it gets a hold on us that we cannot release or refuse. Like I discussed early in *Under Orders*, we have to unearth that part of us in order to know where we're going in life. Otherwise we'll simply wander and never know any particular true way of believing or thinking about God.

Well, this chapter is all about what we believe and where that stuff comes from. Another way to talk about that subject is a process called *hermeneutics* (pronounced "herman-ootics"). This is something studied in universities but which has everything to do with ordinary life. If you learn one sophisticated concept in this book, learn this one. Hermeneutics can change the way you understand things in a powerful way. Don't worry with how funny the word looks, it is worth understanding.

Hermeneutics is the way we go about understanding things. It doesn't just apply to belief systems—hermeneutics can be used for literature and science and most any sort of endeavor where you have to determine what it is that you understand and how you "get there" so to speak. But when it comes to what we believe about God and ourselves, hermeneutics is the most powerful ingredient to that decision. Hermeneutics is the platform for your belief system. It contains all your assumptions about God, the ways you verify God, the mythic hunches you have about the world, and the patterns which you require for believing—each of us seems to have built-in requirements for our belief systems. Our individual hermeneutic lies deep within in our mental thought process and is influenced by how we are raised, by those individuals and events that convey to us what is important and that indicate to us where belief must function. Without even being identified, our perspectives are shaped by all the concepts and ideas that make up our hermeneutic. If your family never went to church your hermeneutic probably excludes all that structured sense of religion described by a particular building or cathedral with pastors or priests and pews and people. You may, because of this, discount the church and not think it factors into your life. By not "developing" in a church growing up then you simply don't have that element in your thinking. That governs your hermeneutic whether you're aware of it or not. Once you realize this you probably need to reassess the entire church thing so that you can insure you're not short-circuiting your available information and resources about spirituality.

Hermeneutics isn't a religious thing in itself, but it does influence every religious thought you have. You can grow up with a benign hermeneutic influence if you have never been challenged to use hermeneutic tools on the engine of your spirituality. Yet once you turn to that part of you which is spiritual, your hermeneutic instantly kicks in and you begin applying your tools. It is an instant thing that few people stop to think about, but it is ever-present. Many people simply go off blindly into religious cults because their hermeneutic requirements are so minimal that if someone tells them they have seen a spirit rising out of the dust, these individuals immediately begin the human spiritual response dictated by that requirement and they worship, somehow, someway.

So, based on how alert you are to your inner hermeneutic, you might be a very religious person or you might be an agnostic.[31] It is all dependent upon your hermeneutic. Let me illustrate with a case example:

I was walking under the camouflage nets of an artillery unit in training one night and came upon a soldier sitting in the darkness taking a break from the operation. He was a young black soldier who seemed ready to talk and engage with me. After just several remarks back and forth I could tell the soldier wanted to elaborate to me the highlights of history and theology as that related to Louis Farrakhan and this soldier's belief in that revisionist history and personal faith. He literally began to espouse his beliefs to me like he was reciting a creedal statement. I couldn't get a word in edgewise. Then he began asking me rhetorical questions about history with themes citing the injustices of white racists and others with respect to the influence of Jews in the commercial and political systems of the government. I would begin to answer and he would halt me and lecture me about my presuppositions. He would ask why I could suggest that the Jewish nation could be believed and why weren't the history books written with the supremacy of the black race as a theme? I rapidly saw that despite what the soldier was saying, his hermeneutic was intolerant. He refused to admit any other ideas could be true. Though his historical references were unofficial, his biases were real clear. His hermeneutic was built upon the assumption that the doing of history (something called historiography by scholars, which he did not know and shook off as insignificant…) was a cleverly disguised process of lying about black people and keeping them as slaves while venerating and elevating the Jewish people. This one assumption guided the rest of his thought process. This process itself known

---

[31] *Agnostic* means you don't know whether God exists or not.

as a "hermeneutic principle" became his guide for every other statement. So as it came to talking about personal faith, God, others, purpose in life, all this soldier's understanding was built on this hermeneutic principle.

Today in the war on terrorism we are seeing the way the Islamic religion is being contorted by dictatorial leaders like Saddam Hussein and fanatical Islamic insurgents so that if you are Islamic the expectation is that you must also war against all Western ideas. And to achieve martyrdom status as an Islamic faithful all you must do is intentionally kill an American or coalition soldier in Iraq. A typical example was a taxi driver who solicited help from American soldiers and ignited an explosion which killed four American soldiers in addition to himself and his passenger. His family received thirty-five thousand dollars from Hussein. He received posthumous medals and religious martyrdom.[32] That was all correct for him, but it was not necessarily right. Plus, his hermeneutic drove his efforts. What he believed and why he believed the way he did governed his actions. For him, that was rightness. But then did he ever examine how he got to that point intellectually? His position was being driven by many assumptions, many of which were not "right" assumptions.

And you and I are the same. Each of us lives according to a hermeneutic principle. We allow and disallow belief according to our philosophic disposition. Now, most sailors and marines don't sit around saying, "Hey, my philosophic hermeneutic says I can't eat normal MREs (meals ready to eat), I need hot chow." But they do say things like, "I'll do whatever the hell I wanna do cause it's my life." That is the hermeneutic at work. Doing what I want to do is a philosophic position. What is then "done" is the result of that position and the choice to execute the philosophy. Many times, a person's hermeneutic principle grows out of desire rather than intellect. If you are interested in prestige, you

[32] Reported openly on CNN, 30 March 2003.

are going to see everything in your life in terms of how you are viewed by others. Therefore, if it isn't cool or snazzy, you won't go for it. And for the most part, most religious stuff isn't cool, snazzy or sought after, so you probably will never embrace religious things unless it is absolutely necessary. And money is a big driver for a lot of people. Money and the love of it provides many people the guidelines for what they will and will not do. So, even though hermeneutics may be very philosophical, it is powerful and driven by very unphilosophical elements inside you.

Everyone has philosophies that guide them. The service tries to assist its member in providing a "utilitarian and military philosophy," which first of all permits things only for the good of the group and things that are inherently positive for good order and discipline. You do not find a consumer philosophy in the military but rather a rigid philosophy. It has to be that way because the military is a regimented and ordered society, which requires members to behave consistently the same, day after day, in order to achieve missions that could not be performed by common civilians.

Once you begin to understand that all groups and individuals have these philosophies you have come to the edge of understanding God better too. Because it is your intelligence that guides you in your beliefs, although it is often distracted by so many other competing feelings and desires. Once you isolate your hermeneutic position you are closer than ever to taking hold of your spiritual life and making it work for you rather than against you. If you try to work with what I'm saying you may find that all the while you thought you were not very religious, you actually were, just in the wrong direction. Maybe your religion, instead of being centered on God is centered on the other "gods" of the world. And you started worshipping those other gods, like girls or guys, automobiles and money simply because you failed to see that your hermeneutics were warped. It isn't your intellectual incapacity to grasp God that is in your way of understanding spiritual things, it is your hermeneutic of what is important. And that drives what you accept. Period. It really is possible to believe and understand God in your life. Let's see how that works.

HOW YOU BELIEVE

Have you realized how many self-proclaimed spiritual advisors there are in the service? Just like barracks lawyers and bedside medics, the religious practitioners are a dime a dozen. There is something "soft" about religious practice that makes it vulnerable to anyone who seems to "understand" it. You've probably seen what I'm talking about. There are individuals who seem to have a seductive and attractive personality with which they assure others of their beliefs. There are certain "signals" to believing their way, which include going to a particular church meeting or group or carrying a particular version of the Bible or some other book written by an "insider" or personality who is also very convincing.

Years ago there was a surge in Evangelical circles where the author was writing about the "last days" of planet earth. Every book he penned was a top seller and his following was quite convinced of his positions. His arguments appeared thoroughly convincing, and with the seven-day war in the Sinai as Israel fought the Egyptians, he managed to create a huge following of upper middle class Americans who looked for the sky to open up and Jesus to come riding in to rescue all God-fearing Evangelicals from high oil prices and anyone who didn't believe in Jesus their way.

And this type of thing is repeated with the types like Louis Farrakhan and the anti-Semitic message he espouses. There is a large military following of all sorts of military men who have embraced a form of Masonic belief and have created a sub-culture of "connectivity" within the military services by which things are done or ignored—all based on your being a Mason or not. I had a sergeant come to me in Hawaii and inform me that his paper-work had been repeatedly lost in the admin section because they were in conclusion, and did not want him to be able to succeed with his career objectives. I have had this happen more than once. Why do service members capitulate to such memberships? It goes back to their hermeneutic. In this case their hermeneutic could be a "disenfranchised hermeneutic" that argues that because the "system" is largely a "white system" it requires I embrace another organization of black individuals that can save me and my career. This could also be seen as a "hermeneutic of struggle" not dissimilar to the Che Guevara type. In Latin America this was seen as what they called Liberation Theology, i.e, the poor of the countries struggled against the political unfairness because the church encouraged them to assert their voice as significant in the economic development of the countries. The church itself took up the mission of struggle against repressive governments that kept the poor of the country out of power because they didn't have the money to oppose the rich. Their understanding of spirituality and God was entirely based in this "struggle" against the government.

There will always be these types of groups, societies and organizations around. They prey on the "unwitting" amongst you. And as long as I've been working in the ministry and in the chaplaincy I've seen them repeatedly surface and I've seen young people march like Lemmings into one lane or another without asking the question of why they are doing it. To ask "why questions" is to get to the heart of what you believe and where you come from hermeneutically. It isn't that hard to ask yourself these questions. It does require courage.

QUESTIONS ABOUT YOUR FAITH

Let's take for example some of the typical questions that seem to surface and let's apply an objective standard to the answers. I will pose a series of questions about religious things and then answer the questions based on this hermeneutic: what is biblical, consistent with history and the church, not racist, and fair-minded. Though I'm a Lutheran, anytime I get "Lutheran" I'll let you know. And as I do this, I assure you that you too can do this process. It is a way of being correct that can lead you to rightness. I won't answer any questions completely, but will answer enough to illustrate how you can believe and where the belief can take you.

Question ONE: Church is irrelevant to me and useless. Fair enough question and often said. Church is an organization composed of like-minded individuals who come together to worship and learn their theological lessons. It is a regular event each week. You do not have to go to church to be a believer but it might be a good idea if you want to develop in your faith. How could you become a skilled skier if you never went to the mountains to ski but just looked at *Powder* magazine once in a while? Another issue about church is the hypocrites who attend there.

It is true that as long as you're looking at church as an organization which is perfect that you will not find any perfect people there and therefore, you will assess it as a bunch of hypocrites. That is your assessment not theirs. Again your hermeneutic says that you think the people there are self-righteous. Actually, church is simply a gathering for those who believe. It isn't supposed to be a fashion show or an elite group. But usually what happens is church has become an organization where there are all the common pitfalls of any other gathering. But judging it because people dress up is rather unfair. People dress up to go to court as well, but that doesn't invalidate the court or the judge who presides there? Is it fair to suggest that they are all illegal who go to court dressed up to gain favor in the eyes of the judge? Perhaps some are, yet the process is greater than the clothes which are worn.

And lastly, there are so many churches, many service members just don't go to any of them because they're all different. Why this opinion keeps people away is anyone's guess. When you're shopping for a new car, you delight in having big dealerships with various deals and offers. Somehow when it comes to churches the idea that there are so many creates this bitterness against the church. Rather than a bad thing, this ought to be a great thing. There is a church for every type and persuasion of belief. And it should be that way because people are different. Some like formality and others informality. Everyone doesn't have to be a Presbyterian or a Baptist, an Evangelical or an Independent. Again, these differences are cultural and hermeneutic. Unless a church simply doesn't believe in the Gospel of Christ, they're pretty much all headed in the right direction with some facets you may like and others you don't like. Don't throw the baby out with the bath water.

Question TWO: **The Bible is too hard to understand.** I agree, it is. But not since the 1950s have we seen a resurgence in the development of Bible study aids and graphics for computer-based reading and study which enhance one's ability to read and understand without having to get a theological degree. Years ago, Gutenberg invented the printing press in the city of Strasbourg (1500s) and he put ink to paper creating the device that transformed modern Bible printing. Before Gutenberg, people didn't have Bibles and they relied on the pastors and priests to tell them what to believe. We are all so much more sophisticated today. We can go online to Bible Gateway, for example, and read to our heart's content all about the Bible and then get commentaries that help to make the Bible come alive both historically and theologically.

There isn't a particular way of understanding the Bible that you need to adhere to. What you should remember is that all "positions" of understanding the Bible are based on a hermeneutic (you learned that already) and many times you will have to sift through a commentator's remarks about the Bible to perceive where they are coming from in their interpretation. Read the parts of the Bible you're interested in and begin with something that doesn't require a degree in Patristics to understand. Read the Gospel of John. It is the simplest and most direct book in the Bible. John was a fisherman and the language that book is written in is some of the simplest Greek construction ever put together. It is a story with a clear point and you learn most of the key elements of belief from a simple person who encounters his savior. You also learn what happens to people who reject the Gospel but who are forgiven. You learn about everlasting life, you learn about friendship and you learn about trust. It is a good news story.

Stay away from the traditionally argumentative and problematic stuff that most people charge into. And once they get embroiled they sour people's impressions of God and religion so that whoever listens to them associates their approach with the Bible. That isn't right at all. Leave the tough parts of the Bible to scholars to "break down" for you. Go to the simplest stuff and start there. The Gospels, Mathew, Mark, Luke and John are still the most foundational books you need to read for your faith.

Question THREE: Who is the Holy Spirit and what are these Gifts about? This topic is one of those which creates more dust than it's worth. Mainly because in the realm of religious experience, people come up with some crazy stuff. You hear reports of nuns seeing visions of Mary in the window of a bathroom and you hear people talk about "hearing the voice of Jesus" when they pray, and you can find people who assure you that once "you know,…you just know." What is that all about? Sounds like an illuminati group. It is the process of experiencing religion and God to these people. And anything goes in this category. I cannot tell you what is right or wrong, or what is legitimate or what is goofy around this globe. I can tell you that you will always have these people in the world and you may be one of them. However, the tradition of this goes way way back in history, it isn't new.

I like to approach this topic by helping you to understand that peoples' experience of God is like viewing a Miro statue. Miro has created a number of these around the city of Chicago. Large beam-like creations look like modernistic creatures who are frozen in time and sandwiched between buildings. But who am I to contest the admirer who thinks these are the feelings of the city or the dreams of the future? Modernistic creations of years ago were always bizarre things we had to suggest meaning for and whose meaning was "untouchable." Many of the current creations are political statements rather than fiction. And when it comes to religion, people still look at religious experience in an "untouchable" category. Because no one can verify what an individual sees or hears, how can you refute what they testify to have seen or heard? You cannot. This goes for all the paranormal and it goes for religion too.

Religions, all of them, have a history of paranormal experi-

ence. The paranormal experience of speaking in other languages and seeing visions is all part of the "phenomenology" of religions. You probably aren't aware of phenomenology and this will be the last time you read about it too, I'm sure. But I'm bringing it up because all religious experience is part of the phenomenon that comes along with believing systems. And because I cannot tell you that you didn't see Mary in the window, you can tell me and everyone else that you did and no one can refute you. However, what does it matter? If you say that you spoke in a "heavenly language" what does it matter? All of these things are simply phenomenon and have little to do with essential core beliefs anyway. You do not have to have an "experience" in order to validate your belief in God. People who suggest to you that the only "real" belief is one which has been proven by something you experience are people who do not trust what they read but only what they "feel."[33]

Contrary to that, our belief in God is something that doesn't need our human experience to validate. Real religion, as the scripture indicates, is one which "helps widows in their time of need." The Apostle Paul had a great deal of difficulty with the Corinthian church because they were "seduced" by the paranormal experience going on in the church at Corinth. Paul suggested to them they start focusing on "hard religion" rather than "soft religion"—my words. Jewish religion and tradition has always insisted that we express our faith more in terms of our actions than our words anyway. Rather than talking about your religious experience, go help someone. That is how you experience God. Plus, how can you really verify whether the experience you have experienced is from God or not? And what does it really matter? Real religion like Jewish tradition and the Old Testament teachings are based in the way you treat your fellow man.

---

[33] This whole subject of the Holy Spirit, the fullness of the Spirit, speaking in tongues, being slain in the spirit, and so forth, are all dimensions of the paranormal which cannot be verified by anyone. Plus, paranormal stuff is experienced in all world religions according to Joseph Campbell and others who indicate that all religions are affected by cultural myths and shared experiences. Read the "Masks of God" series of Campbell for some terrific information about religion and myth. Understanding myth will help you understand why so many service men and women are often swept away by some new trend or idea when in reality, all of these things are old things which like the flu, just keeps going around. Religious experience does not have to be startling or bizarre to be real and influencial.

Question FOUR: Suffering in the world is so great. And always will be. Soldiers die in combat and babies die in the delivery room. Cancer kills indiscriminately and terrorism is rampant in the world. Nothing seems to give us any evidence that God is in this world at all. This is probably the most troubling thing to understand when you are trying to come to belief. And there is no easy answer. I have none. I am daily gripped with the reality of suffering as I watch events unfold in Iraq with the war. I do not understand how a young person who a year previous was feeding animals on a family farm in Kansas is now lying in a pool of his or her own blood in an undescript adobe building somewhere in Iraq. But then that ignores other things that are "higher" than just the bare facts. Those "higher" things I will take up in the next chapter. But the mere facts are disturbing.

The only way I can understand and thus make sense of suffering in the world is to see it in a larger context of meaning. When we see suffering up close it is brutal and sort of sovereign. When a child gets cancer and dies and there is nothing to do but watch their life ebb away, we have to ask ourselves about meaning in our world and how we bring meaning to things like this.

As we have mostly moved away from an agrarian way of life to a technological way of life, we have become quite insulated from birth and death. Death occurs and it is part of life to eventually die. What we have succumbed to is the meaningless of life unless it is lived. Actually, though sickness and tragedy take lives away, nothing can take away the meaning and memory that come with those lives. Our failure comes when we allow the tragedies and loss to dictate to us the nature of God.

It is a common fallacy for people to run up against a tragedy and immediately accuse God of the wrongdoing. It isn't God's fault that tragedy occurs but we make him liable because we are essentially seduced by this idea that we are not responsible for anything that happens. Philosophy calls this "fatalism." I can't do anything about evil in the world so I'm just going to let things happen. God is responsible for the evil in the world, not me. However, this is a childish approach to a more complex situation. Tragedy does exist in the world. Yet according to Christian, Jewish and Muslim tradition, the world is created by God. We on the other hand are responsible for our actions. Evil exists in the world and permeates it. Until this world is transformed it will continue to be essentially evil. Good can permeate times and places in the world and in the midst of chaos, but these will only be glimpses. But the glimpses are often greater than the tragedy itself. Certain intangible qualities like honor, courage and love are always more powerful than suffering, pain and death.

The problem of pain and suffering should not keep you from believing in a God who is greater than this world and who can bring comfort and joy to those who trust and believe in him. Understand that pain and suffering are the result of the evil in the world and that despite the evil the Gospel is capable of bringing hope in the darkest of situations. The pain and suffering question is the hardest of all to handle, and it is understandable if you have difficulty making the intellectual and emotional journey to Gospel because of it. However, you might read the remarks of the Apostle Paul who said that these afflictions of pain and suffering eventually lead to an "eternal glory," which is more significant that the hardship of their results here and now.[34]

I don't usually like to focus on intangible and spiritual results because they aren't very easily understood. But every service member knows what I'm talking about when I say intangible because when you graduate from a course or training you receive a certificate, but you also receive a "sense of pride," which only comes inside. That same sense of spiritual hope is something that you receive in your heart in troubled times. That is why I stress this aspect. We all know how important our inner

---

[34] Paul knew what he was talking about because he was being adjudicated for preaching the good news. He eventually was beheaded for his beliefs in Rome (read 2 Corinthians chapter 4 about "Jars of Clay").

heart is to our perception of things. We also know that we can keep going if our hearts are tuned to the right signal of hope.

Question FIVE: Forms, methods, phrases and patterns. No matter how long you live on this earth, you will find people "promoting" religious ideas, concepts and themes. This book is the same thing. It is sometimes helpful to have a guide to spiritual things, perhaps it helps to bolster your beliefs or assists you in developing a more intellectual faith. And none of this is bad for us. However, when the things that are meant to help us become a substitute for the thing itself, we're in trouble. *Under Orders* is not the end of the matter, only the beginning of a journey.

Some folks are convinced that by saying certain things, repeating phrases, or fully understanding what it is that God wants us to know, that, people are actually saved or born again. And if you look for patterns in the Bible, you're bound to find some. However, there are few "real" patterns in the scriptures like that. The Bible never says you have to do step one, two or three, in order to be saved. There are a variety of scriptural passages that come close to saying that if you do this, then that shall also come about. But more often than not, individuals tack onto the Bible their formulas for believing. It is when that happens that you must beware of the importance placed on the formula or the importance not placed on the believing.

This also applies to Christian living and the "additives" people put onto Christian behavior. Some churches take stands on issues and tell their adherents that if they are truly Christian that they won't do certain things but they will do other things. Well, can that really be the intent of the Gospel? I'm not here to sort them all out and tell you any more than they can tell you, which is the right way to go. What I am suggesting to you is that you examine the things that are being added to your "faith prescription" and be sure that you are believing in the Gospel rather than in the formula.

Anytime you have to say certain words, or pray a certain way, or think a certain way you must beware of the legalistic nature of what is being told you. The Gospel is all about freedom and God's grace to sinners. We will never be much more than sinners so why is there so much fuss over people being righteous. None of us is righteous, "no not one" says Paul in the book of Romans (6:23). How quickly some people seem to take on self-righteous positions as if living a Christian life was easy or something. What we should more be aware of is the overwhelming grace of God, which comes to us as sinners. And it comes best to us when we are fully aware of how miserably worthless we are. Any time I feel I am making progress towards "being righteous" I had better take stock of my life because that is when I've started working my way into the Kingdom of God. God's grace comes to sinners freely. No strings attached.

Question SIX: Emotions and feelings. I have found that most people are completely governed by their inner feelings about spirituality. Most of the service people I listen to are definitely emotional about their beliefs. Few people are driven by intellectual arguments; most are driven by very unsophisticated "feelings" they carry with them in their hearts and minds. The more I talk to people in uniform I find that their religious perspectives are governed by their feelings with respect to parents and upbringing, which shape their views of God. And many of these impressions are viewed as sacred and authoritative for people. In some people, they are very unwilling to alter the way they believe based on this. And so their spiritual life suffers incredibly from a lack of "connectivity."

Think of your spirituality like a "plug-n-play" device. If you start up your computer and shove in the Icard or a USB device, your computer instantly senses something is making contact and it identifies the component, installs what is necessary and boom, things are up and running. Spirituality is like that. It is plug-n-play stuff. But because you might have sour feelings about religion, you never plug yourself into God for that reason. So, you may be the chief blocking agent for a whole new dimension of your life and experience. This is why it is so often that emotional experiences like death and fear often bring people closer to God too. It's not a compelling intellectual argument that will convince your emotions to believe in God, it is going to be the death of your friend in combat, or in an auto crash, which will bring you face to face with the deepest requirements of your soul.

Crisis is one of the most effective ways of getting our emotional center to respond to God. That is why there are no "atheists in foxholes." And yet, after these events are long gone, we still resort to an emotional rejection of God. This yo-yo effect is due to the fact that we are essentially emotional and feeling oriented to God. And if you aren't in a crucible of pain, rejection, dejection, annihilation, adjudication or expiration, you probably don't care about God.

Simply plug-n-play to another level. Feed your mind with reading the Bible and sooner or later you will find it having an enormous effect on your life. Don't simply reject this historic book and its power based on how you feel about it. Let it have its impact on you. Let your emotions follow along as they will but put your mind to the stuff that brings you into contact with the living quality of God's word.

YOUR FAITH

Everyone has some sort of faith. I once said in a chapel service that everyone is at least a theist, a believer in god, and that many people are actually polytheists, or believers in lots of gods. Though we live in a very technologically and informationally "in touch" world, people are still rather "caveman like" in their beliefs. Most people are polytheists. After all, a god is some idea, creature, being or thing, which a person decides to venerate and express feelings of worth towards.

This can be taken to extremes of course. But just think about the things people spend their money to possess, the time they devote to events, and the anxiety given toward health, careers and individuals. By default perhaps, civilizations tend towards venerating many god-like objects. And to some degree in the American society, we venerate the products of our society and the benefits of hard work and reimbursement. None of these things are evil in themselves. As a Lutheran, I rejoice in all the good things God brings to us in this way. However, we should be careful we do not fall perilously into the hands of gods we inadvertently create who cannot save us from our human predicament of sin.

In the Old Testament there is a story of a god named Moloch. It had become routine in Israel for some Israeli families to sacrifice their sons to this Ammonite god. Scholars suggest the ceremony was a sort of ritual where the god was shaped into a furnace=like structure so that the mother and father would walk up to the opening and toss their baby into the mouth of Moloch to sacrifice their child for favor. The prophets of the time rejected the

practice but still some Israelis thought that this was a more effective means of getting God's attention and blessing than following him through the ways of the Law and the Prophets in the synagogues. Of course you can imagine the horrific screams that must have called out from the furnace as the infant writhed in the hell of the flames while the parents felt themselves so much the more religious for having committed their child to Moloch.

Today there is no furnace of Moloch but there are other furnaces where we toss ourselves or our children. Anytime we turn away from the good news of the grace of God, we are turning to the mouth of Moloch for help. But Moloch cannot help us. Only the good news is good. And that news is that regardless of how we feel about faith or have raised or effected, God's forgiveness and life belong to us and our families without charge or requirement. At this point, I'm being very Lutheran now. But that's okay. You should measure your own spiritual viewpoint with mine. I told you early on that part of the process of being spiritually astute is your abililty to understand yourself and how you believe in concert with other viewpoints. It is as important to me that you understand why you might not believe in my Gospel message as to how you believe in what you do hold to as truth.

You see from my viewpoint as a Christian chaplain, each person is spiritual and each person has the power of choice to believe in what he or she wishes to believe. My argument is simple, "Know what you believe and live by it." Yet as you hold to it, do not hold it in a vacuum. You see? Hold your beliefs with credibility by understanding how you believe. I always revert to the image of that young soldier in Somalia puffing on his cigarette and declaring to me how he had figured out God and reality. But his calculations were all done in the safety of his own conclusions. How could he be anything but right by doing that? Of course he was right! In his own mind he was!

That isn't belief. That is ignorance. Believe what you will but believe it after testing it against the fair rules of coherence truth theory, historical information, and its logical coherence with other ideas in the history of ideas. My chaplain assistant astutely observed this in his own church experience where the pastors weren't really theologically trained but were simply well-read in certain phraseologies in the Bible. As a result, when he had a question about theology, the answers all ran in the same direction almost like "proof-texting." Like if he wanted to know about current events in light of the Bible, the answer was always something in terms of Jesus coming again to rescue us from a troubled world. And when he might ask about why the world is troubled, it was because Jesus was coming again. What's missing here? The answer to the issues about the power of sin in human nature and what makes man essentially evil. For someone who isn't read into the historical theology surrounding this, all answers lead back to Jesus the Rescue figure. And that might be okay if you don't want to think much, but when you come into personal crisis and need the answer to why your marriage is failing or your teenager is hurting or why you can't seem to take communion and feel right about it, you need a theological and psychological answer.

Life isn't easy nor are its answers and you will find that being a spiritual being in the world requires you to often struggle to have a proven faith. But that is okay. In my own life I have found that I may not have been assessed as spiritual as other chaplains just because my mind is linked to my faith. Maybe my prayers don't sound as good as the holy words another person can utter. But I know this, my faith has been tried in the vises of intellectual questioning and hammered in the crucible of life's unforgiving events so that I emerge each day more confident in that which I believe. And I also know that as unworthy as I feel to be called a Christian, I am a Christian because of the Grace of God to me, a hopeless sinner. If you are tracking with me then read on.

considerations

Consideration 1: How do you define your theological beliefs? Are you an atheist or an agnostic? Do you hold to a "high" view of the Bible or a "low" view—and do you understand what that means? So many people view Christianity as "generic" in that they figure they know all about it because they grew up in a culture mostly influenced by Christian thought and faith. But this isn't a fair view of Christianity. In order to test your position, articulate your beliefs on paper. Explain God, how you understand God and how God reveals himself in the world to human beings. If you can do this successfully then go further and explain why in Christian cultures redemption is such a key ingredient and how it is reflected in Western values. After finishing that project you should double check your work with the *Dictionary of the Christian Church* from Oxford Press and see how you fare. You will see, it isn't so simple. Having faith is easy, but working out your faith is tough.

Consideration 2: Next is the tough assignment. Write out your hermeneutic method. I figured this might be tough for you so let me suggest you start with stating your cultural assumptions, then move from that to stating your assumptions or claims about truth in the world (this is the philosophic part so you'll have to state what you think is the way reality is figured out in the world, i.e., how do you know if things are really true and if they're true why do they have any bearing on you and me?), then after that exercise move to telling how you read and understand any statement at all from the Bible. After you have accomplished that, read the first chapter of the Gospel of John and answer this: Who is Jesus? Who is God? What is the truth claim stated there? What is man's problem in the world? What is the answer John gives? And how do we know any of this is true?

Consideration 3: I didn't mean to wear you out. Here is your last thought-provoking task. Explain to a friend why you believe what you believe and let them cross-examine you. You'll find this is a powerful way of refining your belief system even if you exit this chapter without Christian type faith, you'll exit more informed about your own faith.

ORDER TEN

Strive for this. Love is the ultimate Law and the beginning of a new world order which begins inside you.

"what you do today will echo into eternity"

from the movie *Braveheart*
Scottish tribes facing a final standoff
against the British Armies

WHATEVER...

It just doesn't seem like anything matters anymore, to some people. However, you can't tell that to Private Lynch, the nineteen-year-old prisoner of war rescued during Operation Iraqi Freedom from a dingy cellar in the dusty, enemy-infected hospital in An Nasiryah, Iraq.

In the chaos of the raid by the special team which extracted her, Private Lynch heard a sergeant call out, "We are American soldiers, here to rescue you and take you home!" Lynch yelled, "I'm an American soldier too!" That moment can be lived by every person in uniform because Private Lynch did what each of us do every day when we put on our uniform and go to work. We are soldiers, sailors, airmen and marines and we are aware of the difference it makes to wear that uniform. Stuff does matter. And that harrowing cellar of the hospital in Iraq showed us that this generation knows the difference between "whatever" and "what else." Once again, being military helps you to understand stuff that isn't as clear to your contemporaries out of uniform.

That cry in the raid should be heard around the world. This generation is capable of remarkable acts of courage and honor under fire. Even as I have penned the chapters of this book we have seen more POWs rescued from Iraq and heard more courageous stories of service people who met the call for courage. Others died in firefights and returned home wrapped in the colors of their country. It all reminds me of the power of this generation and the great job they've done whether on the ground, in the air or on the sea furnishing the support through endless hours of grueling and dangerous work conditions. These are the pride of this book, this generation of service members. Your courage is evident and your capabilities are as strong as any other generation. You can be clear minded about your life and choices. Despite what and how your generation has been labeled, you do know how to make specific and right choices when required to. Sometimes those are difficult to make; but it is my observation that when it comes to crunch time, if you have the information you can determine your choice.

I know you are not ambivalent about your personal faith either. You just might not be too sure how it works yet. Once you figure it out, you'll be making ardent strides in that as well. The power of faith is in its ability to bring clarity and make sense of our lives in the world. In the realm of faith, it is often true that it requires us to take the first step in order to begin the realization process. Like small amounts of morning light, our personal faith ignites an ever widening understanding of spiritual perception the more we allow it room in our minds and hearts.

In this chapter I will talk about Christian faith and how it works for me. This may be somewhat more confessional than the previous chapters. And I do that so that you can take all the tools I've provided you in the previous orders and bring them to bear on this final order of "the Law of Love." I'm not talking about romantic love but of self-less or unconditional love. It is not about your capability to love but about God's capability to love you despite who you are or who you think you are. Note that difference carefully because everything turns not on your ability but God's abilities, which are limitless.

In the end, the good news of the Gospel is not about how holy you can be but how awful a person God can still love and redeem. That Gospel message is pretty powerful and I will attempt to sketch out in this chapter how that message never goes away but always reasserts itself in the problems and predicaments of life. A faulty understanding of Gospel leads to some strange stuff. Remember, from how I understand the Gospel, God never intends you to look any further than his redemption of you for your answers. Any time you start qualifying the Gospel with your accomplishments or behavior you are adding stuff that doesn't belong. Good news is just that, good. And it can't be improved upon with your good works or your failures. Good news stands alone for us as a never ending resource.

A REALLY BAD DAY FOR ANYONE

The Gospel story in the Bible ends tragically with the death of the young Rabbi Jesus at Jerusalem's Golgotha hill, a public area designated for ultimate viewing on a hilltop, the ground littered with the accoutrements of torturous scaffolding, spent rope, large iron nails, and bloodstains on the weeds and rocks below.

On the particular day Jesus died in Jerusalem, the Roman officers in charge of the daily executions rostered a couple of thieves to hang up alongside the young religious claimant. The trial had gone badly with Jesus losing to the bellowing pitch of his own people who did not want to support him. His claims were ridiculous and far-fetched. Nobody could really have survived such a mob mentality anyway. Just the sheer excitement and disruption of the crowd caused Pilate to capitulate to the demands of the Jewish people.[35] Jesus was sentenced to death for supposedly claiming he was the "king of the Jews," something he never claimed but was attributed to him. During his crucifixion, he continued to focus on the good news even to the two thieves alongside him on the hill.

Religious leaders and scholars have made much to do about the last words of Jesus on that hill that day.[36] On the ground the soldiers were doing what soldiers do, making light of the unlucky criminals for getting themselves in such a bind. They suggested that if Jesus were truly a king that he could save himself. They offered him some vinegar and water. We don't know if he opened his mouth to taste it or not. The soldiers were trying to do their job the best they could and make the miserable torture fit the crimes. Just another day at work for them.

As the trio of unlucky criminals hung on the scaffolding known as the cross, a short but intense conversation was struck up between the three. One of the criminals looked over and suggested that if he, Jesus, were truly the "king of the Jews" he should save himself and the two unlucky thieves. The other criminal, perhaps having a bit of fear just in case Jesus proved to be who he said he was, rebuffed the other and asked Jesus to remember him when Jesus came into his kingdom. And the answer was full of Gospel, "I tell you the truth, today you will be with me in Paradise" (Luke 23:43). That "deathbed" conversation

---

[35] The crowd had become enraged at the rabbi Jesus and were willing to negotiate an exchange of the prisoner Barabbas for him at this kangaroo court with Pilate. Pilate, the governor of the area, was acting on tradition when he allowed for the exchange, otherwise he might have protected Jesus as a prisoner. There were no civil charges levied against the rabbi. This was religious zealousness which appealed to the occupying Army force and won.

[36] The seven last words of Jesus are the seven last phrases he speaks. You will find in that last event of Jesus' life all the important things you ever wanted to know about life, death and spirituality. Plus, if you read all 4 Gospel accounts you will see a slightly different perspective on the same situation and words.

stands out in scripture with such clarity that it makes understanding spiritual things really easy. If we ask for grace we get it
without conditions and requirements—it is free.

It affirms the bottom line about the ultimate law of love.
God's love isn't about what we can contribute to make our case
look good to God, but what his love can do to make us who look
pretty bad to be included in the kingdom of God.

Now I don't think the two thieves positioned next to Jesus
that day were good people at all. In fact, I have to believe from
the account that they had been repeat offenders, who had broken Jewish laws and/or Roman civil laws and had ended up
without any possibility of rehabilitation or redemption. These
guys were at the end of their ropes, literally!

Despite the difference in culture or historical setting, we all
seem to find ourselves hanging at one point or another between
our failures and intentions without a prayer to hold onto. It is at
those times we need to hear the Gospel message clearly. To those
who want or ask, they will receive the absolution, the forgiveness, the entrance to new life, without anything more than a
right attitude. But it has to be wanted to be received.

So, the good news for a really bad day is that whatever God's
love is about, at the end of the story about Jesus, there is still this
unconditional favor to people who "don't have a prayer" to
escape the penalties of a wasted life.

Gods, gods and more gods

Not everyone believes in God nor does everyone believe in
the story of a person named Jesus who died on a cross in
Jerusalem—a common criminal execution turned a mystic
moment of redemption for millions. But most consider Jesus to
have at least been a remarkable prophet and for millions in the
world, he is generally accepted to be God's Son, come to earth
to proclaim the good news of salvation.

Despite what I might argue about Jesus, there are many
service members reading this who would just as soon declare

the story of Jesus a fable, a cleverly concocted story to promote this incredible God-man idea and be the myth of two thousand years of religious admiration, controversy and division. Well, rather than take the time to talk that piece, let me suggest that if you hold to that position that you take time to think through other ideas about man and his condition. Put your intellectual powers to work on ideas other than the Gospel and see if they can bear up to the same scrutiny with which you might discount the Gospel's authenticity.

People really do encounter insurmountable obstacles in life. Disappointment and disillusionment in life lead people to seek resolution and comfort. God isn't an idea outside the boundaries of our thinking. The idea of god is inherent in the human myth in all cultures. As I said before, all cultures have religion as part of their makeup. These religions vary, and even in American culture there are many gods, not just Baptist, Presbyterian and Lutheran gods, there are lots of gods. We just don't think about god they way god might want to really be thought of, rather, we think of god as only in terms of churches when we ought to be thinking of god as something or someone we are crazy about. When you open up your concept about god you will find that there are many gods. We should be asking ourselves whether the god we say we believe is a real God.

Our culture is as polytheistic as Indian culture yet we don't see ourselves that way. Polytheism is the belief that there are many gods rather than just one god. In the Hindu religion there are hundreds of thousands of gods. Their understanding or portrayal of god is in those terms and so they really never think about a monotheistic or single god idea. But Hinduism does not have the same concept about a personal faith and the development of a relationship with God. After all Hindus believe in successive reincarnation of a life until it reaches a point of Nirvana. But that concept doesn't answer the spiritual mail for American service people struggling with questions about ultimate reality, death, fear and relationships—all justified and authentic issues.

And Hindus don't allow for personal integration of faith with God. Remember, *Under Orders* is all about how you can begin to understand your faith, whatever it is, and develop a relationship with God personally. My approach is based on the Gospel message in which Jesus dealt with individuals directly about their failure and their redemption. My issue is not with the validity of other religions but of the significant originality of the Gospel for your personal requirements today. If you think it is audacious to talk about a faith which delivers "salvation" to you personally, then the Gospel isn't for you. There are plenty of gods out there willing to be yours. However, not many have any power other than that which you give them.

Our modern techno culture is full of digital gods, transportation gods, relational and emotional gods, chemical gods and so forth. The polytheism of India is similar to that of the Western world except that Western culture does not see its worship as religious, but rather as obsession. My argument is that we are essentially polytheistic whether we consider that religious or not is a moot point. Service men and women know the power of the gods of this world and know that when it comes to crunch time that a more powerful god is needed to break through and give them peace and assurance.

SLEEPING GODS

Most people in American culture think there's only one God though they live like there are lots of gods.[37] Most American young people act and respond to the whims of the gods they worship and are unresponsive to the God of the Universe. Gods like consumption, control, power, greed and possession are amplified by passion, greed, envy and uncontrolled desire. These

---

[37] This is the age old concept of monotheism and polytheism. Once again, the structure of the word describes the meaning, poly + theism = many + gods = polytheism. Atheism is a (which is a negative) + theism = no + gods = atheism. What would pantheism be? Answer: everything + gods = gods everywhere.

are then channeled through the capacities of our intellects, sexuality and purpose, so that our entire lives become the vehicle of our gods. Someone whose god is power then subjects everything in their life to power. There is no morality to the god nor anything which can stop this god. Not only does this god lack a moral framework, this god is as powerful as we let it become.

We discussed this in the last chapter in terms of the god of Moloch. My issue with this concept of gods is, "What good are they?" If I believe in a god who doesn't benefit me, alleviate my personal sorrow, or fails to provide me hope, then what good is that god? What good is a god whom I have constructed in my own mind or by my own suspicion? And what good is a god which exists only as a result of my own agenda, only to serve me and my ends?

If you recall the order about interpretation you will realize that lots of people believe in gods that have no rational validity simply because they want to "feel" strongly about their ideas rather than engage with the God of the Gospel. These aren't real gods, these are simply imaginary ideas to promote my own wants and desires in this life. They will die with me.

In the Christian view of the world, the fact that there are many gods is a given. However, that doesn't mean that Christian theology accepts any of those gods as capable of performing what human beings need in their lives. Gods are any object or thing we choose to be the driving force for our lives, the meaning of our lives. On the other hand if we are choosing the god and that god is material then all that god becomes for us is a thing-god. I would add that a god must meet the tough criteria of being capable to deliver. After all, the word *god* presupposes almightiness, transcendence, timelessness and omnipotence (all powerful). Although many gods are chosen by people today, they are simply objects of pursuit rather than true "gods" that can interact with our little lives here in this life. Like Elijah commented on Mount Carmel to the prophets of the god Baal,

"Maybe your god is sleeping."[38] If the gods you have chosen either willfully or by default, due to your obsessions or desires, cannot help you when you cry out to them then what good are they to you. They must be sleeping gods.

In addition, there is another problem that Christian thinking addresses and that is the problem of mankind's "judicial" problem. Each man has an essentially "legal" kind of problem with sin, which grows out of the concept of the Fall of man in the garden of Eden. We looked at that theological story in Order Six. That Fall passed on to all people the incapability to perform guilt-free. In Christian terms, "All people have sinned," according to the Law. And that is the reason there is a cross in Jerusalem and a Jesus dying for sins. Theologically it is imperative. If there is a Garden of Eden where mankind "fell" into the status of being sinners, there had to be a cross where mankind was provided "redemption" of sins. And what gods cannot accomplish, Jesus did accomplish by this one act of powerful selfless commitment. Despite whether you believe in this "judicial problem" of mankind or not, sooner or later when you need to resource your life in crisis, you will need something to help you with your life, your childrens' lives or the events this life brings to us every day.

LAW AND GOSPEL

Early on in this book, I spoke about the tendencies of young service personnel to sort of blindly enter the service and, if not cautious, become very much what they were before they entered the structure of the military. Each of us brings a different perspective and experiences to the military and we know that

---

[38] This remarkable account in the Bible in 1 Kings illustrates the power of a real god in contrast to a mentally concocted god. It illustrates that a God must be interactive in order to be authentic. It is one thing to claim you follow something in contrast to believing in a God who can deliver power to the events of our lives in response to our prayers.

despite our differences, the military judicial code is consistent and requires the same of all of us. It is very similar to the Law of the Jewish people. I am referring to the Law in the Jewish sense of the word as the Torah and which generally refers to the regulations and requirements upon which the Jewish scholars and teachers based their religious tenets. In the military system our law is the Uniformed Code of Military Justice (UCMJ). We discussed this briefly on the chapter about sin. Most of us have some sort of moral upbringing that conveys to our conscience what right and wrong is. In addition, some may have more definition about that in terms that their family provided or in terms of their particular faith and belief system.

The fact that there is this concept of Law provides us the baseline to understand human failure and redemption. The bottom line is that the Law illustrates to us how we have participated in the human drama of sinfulness by being part of the human race. When Adam sinned in the Garden of Eden, we sinned with Adam judicially. Because he and Eve "fell" from the Grace of God at that time, so we also by being human beings receive the same failure status.

On the other hand, because of the Gospel, we see that regardless of what gods we might depend on and what deeds we may have committed, God is always willing to wipe our judicial record clean and start our lives over again for good. This is a very liberating feature of Christian faith.

As a Lutheran Chaplain, I encounter many service people who live under a law of some sort or another. And those who are religious many times live under more rigorous laws than those who are not. It is my view of scripture and the world that each person lives under the "penalty" of breaking the Law in that they participated in humankind's original sin in Adam.[39] And law includes this frustrating feature that does not require you to be present in order to validate that you have "broken a law." As we

---

[39] Order Seven talks about this concept of "original sin."

hear said time and again, "ignorance of the law is no excuse for breaking a law." Laws exist and in the conventional world, we are obligated to be apprised of these laws so that we do not break them. However, when it comes to the age old problem of sin, people are not so happy to accept the fact that they have broken God's laws. Yet by simply observing people it is apparent that they are lawbreakers by their actions.

When the Jewish legal scholar Paul wrote the book of Romans in the New Testament, he made the statement that "we know that everything in the Law applies to those who live under the Law, in order to stop all human excuses and bring the world under God's judgment" (Romans 3:19). This legal argument implicates all people and suggests that no matter if we are witting or not, the intent of the law is to put a stop to "human excuses" about sins and sinning.

Most of us think of the Ten Commandments when we think of Law. Actually the Jewish people used them as their central document but added to them many thousands of ceremonial and procedural laws so that if you were a traditional Jew, you had much more to be concerned about than just a code of ten items.

But for the sake of argument and clarity to what we're tackling in this chapter, think about Law just in terms of the ten laws of Exodus 20, which begins with Law number one: "I am the Lord your God who brought you up out of Egypt…Worship no god but me." I don't need to elaborate all ten of this Law document in order to illustrate that the core feature of the Ten Commandments is that the Jewish people were to worship only one God and that God is described in the history of the Jewish people as a God who delivers them from the oppression of the Egyptians.

As you have learned to do in *Under Orders*, set aside your biases and prejudices for a minute, disregard Jewish and Egyptian and focus on the monotheistic theme of the Law. *No other gods* is the prohibition. How many of us can really admit that we are monotheistic and worship the God of the history of the Bible? Well, for some the Bible may present a hurdle that has to be looked at. For others it is an issue of the fact of the worship of just this One God which becomes a problem. Especially in this polytheistic techno world we live in.

Plus, many more service men and women don't even include God into their category of needs and requirements. After all, why bother about God when you can't see god and you don't really care about religion? Well, it goes back to the simple assumption in this world expressed by experience and verified by biblical facts that to make sense of the world, one has to understand the sin factor in the world. If you know of any other story that adequately purges the human being from the worries sin brings, then you need to market it. At this point, the story of redemption as typified in the God-Man Jesus dying on the cross is probably the only event and story that brings to culmination all the pain and suffering of mankind into one redemptive moment and liberates people based upon the sheer goodness of God, which again the Lawyer Paul says, "leads us all to repentance" (Romans 2:4). And this is the secret of the new Law: it is God's goodness which leads us to repentance, or changing our mind about God. This one fact is the new paradigm of the Gospel, which makes this order the most powerful of all in this book.

Living and understanding God is not some additional form of legalism or set of requirements that holy people put upon themselves to get God's favor because there is no favor to get this way. The point here is that goodness is what God is all about, not Law.

A NEW ORDER WITHIN YOU

With the turn of the millennium and the changing world situation you might think that there are new sets of spiritual rules that also apply to this world. I disagree. I think that the "new" in this world is the new language that we have to use to start describing how God works in the world with us. Due to the fact that God really never changes, that we change instead, the requirement that remains is to discover how to articulate God in the language of the present. The traditional scriptures of the Old Testament provide images and understandings of God as both a God of Law and a God of Grace. These concepts go hand in hand in any good understanding of theology and the person of God's nature. However, the problem is most often with the Law rather than grace because most people naturally feel guilty about the Law whereas they lack the capacity to understand how God can be so gracious as to forgive them for their sins. This lack of understanding continues throughout peoples' lives despite the constant attempts of ministers to try to untie the mental confusion of some individuals.

It is easier to understand how God can find us guilty than to understand how he could forgive us. The new order is understanding the role of God's grace in our lives as opposed to his Law.

So what does the goodness of God mean? And why should it be more important than the Laws of God?

The first impact of God's goodness is that the message of the Gospel is about good for you. Not about bad. It isn't the intent of the biblical message to condemn anyone. The Gospel is for people who realize that their life is deleted, toast, terminated or discontinued, so to speak. When you come to the point where you are struggling to understand why and where things went wrong, the Gospel is meant to give you a word of hope and significance that brings new order and life to you. All those Bible stories aren't just for Sunday school, they're for people struggling to understand the person of God. You meet God face to face in the stories. Too much of religion confronts searching service members with regulations and restrictions. Now it might be that if you adopt the Christian way of life that you may terminate some habit you have, but that is up to you and God. If you can break away from your misconceptions about religion and start to confront the actual message being presented you will realize that faith in God is all about God's goodness to you rather than what you can do for God.

Secondly, the goodness of God impacts on people who are already trying to live religious or spiritual lives. The impact is that living a life of worshipping God is not about becoming like someone who carries a Bible in your wing, your battalion, or battle group aboard a ship. It is about you feeling at ease in the world God has created. All things God has created are good and are meant for your enjoyment.[40] Luther believed that all life is sacred. If you start "reframing" your way of looking at the world you'll begin to see that knowing God is more about validating God than you trying to figure God out. People who have to "work" issues related to believing in God are often also people who begin to put all sorts of "conditions" on God's grace. Suddenly their understanding of God is more about attendance at church, reading a certain book, or saying certain religious phrases than it is about enjoying the world God has made.

I find this a rampant epidemic in the Army world. A recent example is a young sergeant who found some sort of excitement in praying and speaking in "tongues" (not that I can verify whether any of what he is doing as being real or not!). He had learned some Pentecostal phrases and came into the installation chapel every morning to chant and burble in unintelligible syllables as if he had found the secrets to a phenomenal spiritual life. To me it was obvious that he had been "schooled" by a strand of people who are devoted to living Christian lives according to a certain model. But when I look objectively at this individual I realize that he actually possesses some obvious talents of persuasion and uses them to his advantage in his pursuit of God. It is his own "experience" of God rather than God himself that he is following. And one could say that the only thing he has found is really a picture of himself as a Pentecostal doing these things he thinks are spiritually beneficial! But he doesn't view it that way I'm sure. What will happen the day he realizes that this little God-Experience-Play is simply an acting out of a

---

[40] This comes from the Heidelberg Catechism of Martin Luther. Good reading for you if you want to dig deeper. Don't assume you know anything, read and discover what is out there to understand.

psychology of his own religion? Can I tell him to read William James on the *Varieties of Religious Experience?* Probably not. Most people who claim to experience God are also extremely jealous of their experiences. It often requires the individual to "sin" gravely before he or she returns to a state of normalcy, or, to depart from their faith. And then they announce how religion never works for them when in truth, they never encountered Christ but some clever sayings or rules that camouflaged the Gospel. They should be upset that they got sidetracked and misled. But they should also return to the good news of the Gospel and see it without their limitations and regulations.

In another instance an individual like this sergeant had to "fall away" from his faith by embracing his homosexuality and divorcing his wife before he realized that he had been "play acting" a spirituality that didn't have any impact on his life. My recommendation for people who are trying so hard to be religious is that they stop completely and give up. If you think you can achieve spirituality by doing anything more than receiving God's free grace you are mistaken.[41] If you didn't do another thing from here to the day you die, you would still be saved by the Grace of God. When even well-meaning people add their assertions and limitations to the Gospel they add to the Gospel and it becomes their Gospel, not God's.

Lastly, the goodness of God is the Gospel. I think it is one of the tricks of the Devil that people are led to believe that knowing God is a complex and stressful experience that requires so many echelons of excruciating personal agony and revival and progress. I don't discount that oftentimes our lives are filled with much of these. But it is untrue to describe the Gospel in any terms other than liberation.

---

[41] Martin Luther spoke of this in terms of "sinning boldly" because anyone who thinks that he or she can enter the Kingdom of Heaven because of their own righteousness, no matter how cleverly conceived is clearly misled. Luther says that if we are going to sin we shouldn't be discrete but "sin boldly" in order to understand the grace is completely from God alone. And then we can repent and turn completely to Christ.

The Good News of this Order is that the goodness of God leads us to change our minds about God. Repentance isn't a soul charring experience but a mental readjustment by which we change our thinking about God. Literally, it is a change of mind. I stress it this way because people tend to use their own metaphoric language about these things, which in turn begin to take on urban-legend sorts of understanding. Sometimes these terms like "baptized by the Holy Spirit" or "slain in the spirit" or "re-baptized" or "born again" represent a mental and spiritual obstacle course of terms which get in the way of people understanding the simplicity of the Gospel. Once made complex, then rules and working for your spirituality begins and it is no more grace but performance that is your salvation. Once there, you cannot say you understand the Gospel correctly.

Many of us who are Christians already probably need to readjust our thinking about the Gospel even today. Others who are just realizing the Good News need to always keep in mind that Good News is never improved upon and it is always good. When I talk with service people, I find them hesitant to attempt attending church or being more "religious" but few understand the liberation of the Gospel. Most find anything having to do with religion like a death sentence. In addition, most interpret religion and the Gospel as one and the same. So the Gospel gets a bad review by people from religion and in so doing, few look at it for any benefit.

If I could say one thing in *Under Orders* it would be that everything that has to do with God is good news instead of bad news. But that is easier said than done.

A FINAL WORD

Well, you have trudged through ten tough orders and lots of considerations. *Under Orders* is meant to challenge your thinking so that you will be able to put together the elements of your faith journey. In this last segment I turn to the subject of the

Good News itself asking the question why is it good news? And why does it matter to me? I figure if you've made it this far, it does mean a great deal to you. If for no other reason, the answer to good news at least helps us understand the essential part of the Gospel story. If you begin with the good news you cannot go wrong. And if you start from there and understand the Gospel you have a great start at building a firm foundation on a Christ-oriented concept of faith. And from there, you have a better understanding of religion too. But everything must begin with the Gospel in my opinion.

Christ didn't come into the world to condemn the world but that through him the world might be saved. Saved from what? Saved from being redundant and meaningless, that people might have lives of significance and meaning rather than emptiness and sorrow. This is not about reviving religion, this is about returning to the foundations of religions' attempts to convey some news the world at large does not possess or promote. If you are disappointed with the state or condition you see in the church, join the club. Many of us want to see change in the church and the world but that is the global level of the impact of the good news. The place where the Gospel is supposed to impact is firstly on the lives of individuals who come into contact with it and then it will impact in greater ways.

And the Gospel is usually carried along not on the back of an intellectual argument but on the merits and actions of individuals who have been impacted. The Gospel is a living thing, it's not a philosophic concept. The new order of Gospel to your world comes when individuals who have been in contact with the Gospel meet you and bring the aspects of forgiveness, understanding, healing and compassion to you.

Service members usually find some sort of religious experience through another individual. That person might be influential for one reason or another, none of which might be either religious or right! But people are influenced by people! The Gospel has always been meant to be understood in terms of people. This is a common thing and occurs with most things in life. People seem to trust people when it comes to recommending things, products, events and ideas. However, once we are referred to a car dealership where another soldier found such a good deal, we always look at the product, scrutinizing and analyzing to get just the right thing for ourselves so that we don't waste any money. Why is it that when it comes to religion we don't do the same thing? Just because somebody in your wing decides that going to such and such a church is such a great thing doesn't mean that you

 shouldn't investigate the doctrine of that church or ask questions about the nature of the religious practice that is occurring there? Just because someone says you ought to speak in tongues, don't you think it a good idea to investigate what this is and where it fits in the larger picture of faith and religious experience? Some of these claims and positions are filled with hidden requirements that do not correspond with the Gospel of Christ.

A good many service people would save themselves much time and effort in personal and spiritual matters if they'd only look at the product people are espousing. Look at the Gospel factor. Determine the religious and spiritual bottom line that individuals claim. If it involves good news and sharing that good news, it is probably good for you. However if it involves steps, levels, meetings and processes that involve your straining to attain a level of competency in religious matters, no matter how spiritual they may sound, you might want to look at your friend's faith or church, or group one more time. People often influence people but not always for good. I see this most often in the military where service folks on deployments and operations find themselves constrained to listen to barracks pastors who hold others captive to their ideas however proven or un-proven they might be. This isn't news, this is old stale stuff that anyone can read or reproduce given enough time and practice and people skills of persuasion. But that isn't Gospel, that's manipulation.

The Gospel is good *news*. It is news! And because it is news it is something announced to you. It isn't earned or qualified for, it is news to you. When we flip on the television we get the news. When we encounter the New Testament message of Christ, we are getting the good news. It is declarative in nature. In other words, this is news you may not have known, which is full of impact for you. It has the endorsement of the same individual who said to that thief on the cross at Golgotha, "Today you will be with me in Paradise." That was sure good news. The unlucky individual had crossed the legal line too many times and had run out of second chances. It is that individual who received "good news" that day. And that model, contrary to all other models I discussed earlier, is a model which can always be relied upon. The product is a news item, a news for you that is the forgiveness of your sins despite what has happened to you in your life. Some people live for years in a state of holy fear that because they have committed a particular sin, God will no longer forgive them. Others may live in fear that the sin committed against them by a sodomizing parent will never be forgiven. Others live in emotional paralysis brought on by harassment, judgment and unforgiving parents. Wives live under threat of mistreatment, the subjects of unloving husbands who torture their emotional fragility, which in turn causes them to believe their duty is to love and honor that individual despite his raging beatings. I have encountered many soldiers in my travels in the military who relay to me horrific stories of personal tragedy and disappointment only to not believe God can ever forgive them for their encounter with some unholy thing, event, time, place or person. This is not true. The good news is declarative, "Today you will be with me in paradise," Christ says. Think of the good news of Christ to you today as, "Today you will be forgiven in full…today you will no longer bear the feelings of unforgiveness….today you will be free."

The most powerful aspect of Good News is the fact this declaration of news to me and you is that despite our essentially evil nature, God forgives us our sins *in full* with no expectation of duty, payment or obligation in return. And you're thinking, that's too easy—too good to be true. I know it seems that way. And I know that those who are most guilty always feel that forgiveness like this is too generous and that it cannot be authentic. But that's not your call is it? The good news does not need your qualification or your limitations. Part of the powerful aspect of the good news is that it is news which is being broadcast to you, not being invented by you. And the other powerful aspect is that it is good. For you to revise the good news as incapable of resolving your lifelong guiltiness is your effort to reduce Gospel into a form of penitence, which it is not.

So the ultimate law isn't a law at all, it is some really good news about God for you that comes in the message of forgiveness for us regardless of offense and irrespective of the weight of sin's guilt on us. This Gospel is "in effect" in this world today. It comes without any conditions attached to it. But it isn't for everyone. Only those who are waiting for something better than what they presently have and know.

Looking back over all the soldiers who have passed through my influence and advice, it is like a sort of parade of situations in which the service member feels that he or she is the only one to ever experience the problems, the heartaches, the disappointments and the rejections they share with me. However, from my vantage point, it is very different. The problems change in terms of the people's names and the times of the events but the problems are identical. And this one characteristic seems to stump most of those who seek solutions, that their life isn't unique after all, it is common. And yet the uniformed person often seeks some advice only to wander still further from the news that could benefit them the most.

considerations

Consideration 1: Thinking through the concept of news and the generic meaning attached to it. If God has "Breaking News" available, why aren't you investigating it? Remember, the Gospel is "new" to each individual. Though the Gospel story can be told ten thousand times over again, when you hear it, it may be the only time you will hear it. Have you ever heard about people who said, God spoke to them? Well, that same concept may apply to your hearing of the good news. And if you're "hearing" something in the Gospel, that news is "breaking news" for you. Have you heard the news God has for you or are you still bleary-eyed when you hear faith stories? Perhaps you should ask God for some assistance in "hearing" the news he has for you?

Consideration 2: Are you living in the Gospel or in the Law? Do you hold to certain steps, methods, spiritual prescriptions that tell you what you should pray, what you should say, or when you should do any of them? These are legalistic things that people put on the Gospel. Beware of the tendency of influential individuals in your military unit who claim to be "pastors," "elders" or "brothers/sisters." More often than not, these persons possess a certain personality talent to influence but lack sufficient breadth of experience and knowledge of God and the scriptures to truly guide anyone. They are many times self-proclaimed persons or a group has pronounced their title. Like the Staff Judge Advocate lawyers (SJA), for legal problems, and the medical doctors, for health, of the services, see a chaplain for a focused, balanced and fair view to help you in your spiritual quest and journey. Do you know the signs of heresy? Often heresy begins in the untrained minds of good people. Consider Aryanism, which was named after Arian, the good-hearted promoter of the idea of Christ as not fully being God. After the Council at Nicea, Arian was pronounced a heretic. Are you heretical? You may never realize until too late. Think of those things you are promoting and the people you may be influencing today and be careful you are not like Arian.

Consideration 3: What did the thief have to do to be "in Paradise"? The intent of the scriptures is clear, formulism is not the Gospel. Anytime someone tries to package salvation like a "hot pocket burrito" they are running the risk of complicating a simple message. Read Matthew, Mark, Luke and the Gospel of John, and then see how the Gospel is made simple. You can't go wrong reading the Gospel itself! Always keep Gospel in the forefront of your Christian thinking and values.

EPILOGUE

And so, I finish where I left off—with Jenny, the accidental counselee, because she really didn't want help with her life or her problems, she really only wanted help to maneuver around the guidance of her unit. She left without ever having done any self-assessment and without ever finding out why she couldn't get the good news. She was too intent on writing her own life story, stories which most always end up in short-term satisfactions and long-term disappointments. Jenny represents the majority rather than the few who seek and find the good news is really for them.

Traditionally, the military is the place where most postmodern military service members wander away from good news. American youth are more interested in status than in service, in personal desires rather than corporate values, and in what they get rather than what they give. Then there are the exceptions, like those young leaders on Roberts Ridge, or like young Sergeant Streucker on the streets of Mogadishu, or like the young soldier I met the other day who said when asked to describe herself, "dependable, hardworking and honest." There are bright stars in the midst of this military community at the lowest levels and at the highest.

As a young Army Battalion Chaplain I had two stellar leaders who attended my services and supported my effort to spread the good news to the soldiers. One was Command Sergeant Major Jesse Laye and the other was Lieutenant Colonel Paul Eaton, (now Major General Eaton). By supporting my religious mission with their attention and their support, I was able to reach out in unique ways to influence soldiers for good. They believed in the significant role of spiritual stability for young soldiers and though they couldn't perform the function themselves, they supported me wholeheartedly in order to ensure I was able to impact soldiers every day. Today, as I write this epilogue I am concluding my tour of service with the notable 1st Armored Division whose Commander, Major General Martin Dempsey and my Division's Support Commander, Brigadier General Mark Hertling, exhibit the very same characteristics of leadership with spiritual integrity. They support my efforts as a chaplain to bring this good news to soldiers.

The military is beginning to exhibit a host of leaders like these individuals who are the bright stars in a vast system of procedures and regulations where it takes persistence and courage to reach out and care for service members. They do it. And they facilitate religious ministry to these young people too. It won't always be that way in life for you. You won't always have such support in your life. You won't always have leaders who insist on making good things happen for their personnel.

It takes courage of convictions for people to do what is right and for people to make better decisions in their lives. The most opposition you will ever face will be those in your own circle of influence. Remember, it isn't up to you to save the world, that's not your mission. Your mission is to "hear the good news." Don't be too quick to think that everyone needs to hear your news—hear the good news and begin living the liberated life God has for you.

It is time for a change in the way we understand faith in our world. It is time we begin emphasizing the good news over "some" generic news. The Gospel liberates people from the sin of religious regime, boredom, routine, sectarianism and legalism. I don't want a good news if all it is for me is some additional "tasking" I have to do today. I don't want it if it is only something that requires me to speak differently, or look differently. The Gospel comes as light into dark minds and as a new perspective into dusty minds clouded by traditions, misinformation and "old wive's tales" and challenges us to "be different" by being transformed by it. And it comes differently to each of us so that the light God brings can light each of us in the world in various places.

It is time for your generation to begin speaking the Gospel in a new language, which energizes faith by praying, worshipping and talking about God in today's language rather than the language of the past. But that can only begin as service members like you begin taking the Gospel seriously as news for your life and breaking the patterns and structures which block its power from reaching you. Don't settle for accepting what everyone around you tells you is the "way" you should live and believe. Discover the good news for yourself. And then articulate it yourself.

Last of all, these orders are only a guide to help you unwrap some of the common misperceptions about religion, faith, understanding and the simplicity of the good news. If you see them as a jumping-off place you have rightly understood the book. This is only a beginning for you. If you have further questions or you would like to know more about any facet of how you can experience faith or clarify faith in the military environment you life in, please don't hesitate to email me at **admin@underordersonline.com** and I will answer your questions to the best ability I can. In some cases I will refer you to someone smarter than I who can take you the rest of the way.

Our world has changed forever with the dawning of this new millennium and the debut of the cowardly terrorist. That change affects each of us every day. For me today, it takes on new meaning as my sons enter the battle-space again in different modes of operations, one with the Marines and the other with the Special Operations community. And there are a host of parents out there whose children also share in this enormously dangerous campaign. It is important that we hope and believe in good news for this world. And it is important that we do this individually. I believe in the things I write and I seek to live them. I encourage you to do the same.

ABOUT THE AUTHOR

Chaplain (Major) Bill McCoy now serves as the Campus Chaplain to the Command & General Staff College at Fort Leavenworth, Kansas.

He has been Ordained in Ministry since 1977 and has published numerous articles in theological journals and professional magazines.

His formal education has been at the Lutheran Theological Southern Seminary in Columbia, South Carolina (M.Div), and at the Protestant Faculty of the University of Strasbourg France (Ph.D.). He is Ordained by the South Carolina Synod of the Evangelical Lutheran Church in America (ELCA).

He comes from a military family, his father served in the Infantry and the Armor, notably in both the European Campaign of the 2nd World War, and the Korean War. His oldest son is a Platoon Leader with the the 1st Marines. Another son is an Air Force Pararescueman serving with the special operations community. His daughter serves as a telecommunications specialist with the Coast Guard.

Under Orders
Order Form

If you are interested in ordering *Under Orders*, you can do so by completing this form:

Name: _____

Address: _____

City: _____ State: _____

Zip: _____ Telephone: (_____) _____

Number of copies: _____

Price/copy: $12.95

Shipping: $3.95 for the first book and $1.95 for each additional book to cover shipping and handling within US, Canada, and Mexico. International orders add $6.95 for the first book and $2.95 for each additional book.

Credit Card Information:

Card #: _____

Exp. Date: _____

Signature: _____

Make your check payable and send to:
Pine Hill Warehousing & Distribution
85334 Lorane Hwy.
Eugene, OR 97405

or have your credit card ready and call toll free
1-866-301-7323